THE DANCE OF INTERACTION

BY JEANINE FITZGERALD

Personality
INSIGHTS
PRESS

Personality
INSIGHTS
PRESS

ISBN: 0-9741760-7-9

Second Edition: March, 2006
Third Edition: June, 2007

Printed in the United States of America

TABLE OF CONTENTS

DEDICATION

To my parents and brother for teaching me the meaning of family and unconditional love.

To my husband and children for whom you are and all the lessons learned in the field about relationships, commitment and the blessings of parenting.

To my mentor, Janice Caputi, who was a strong advocate and leader in the lives of children and families. She taught me professionalism and her integrity was evident in all our interactions.

FOREWORD

Over the years we have trained close to one thousand consultants who are now using Personality Insights' material. Our three-day consultant training programs are always great times together. We have people from all walks of life come through training: business owners, teachers, pastors, psychologists, counselors, parents, coaches and other professionals. It is always a wonderful experience to see how such a diverse group can come together and stay focused on one topic for three days. The D-I-S-C Model of Human Behavior certainly transcends many boundaries and gives a wide variety of different professions opportunities to learn and grow.

We did not realize it at the time, but several years ago, a very special individual walked through our doors. Jeanine Fitzgerald came from Boston (in New England) to Atlanta (in the South) in order to attend our training. You probably could not find two accents any more diverse anywhere in the country. The New England "twang" and the Southern "drawl" are always an interesting combination! It did not take us long to realize that Jeanine was actually in a class all her own. As a licensed, professional therapist, she knew much more than the average person walking in our door. As time passed and as discussion in class proceeded, we began to see the awesome understanding that Jeanine had concerning people. One thought that she shared became a pivotal point in all of our training. She explained to us that the reason the DISC model is so effective is because it was originally based on a wellness model. Most other models of human behavior are based on a deficit model of behavior. However, the DISC model is based on the emotions of normal people. When Dr. William Moulton Marston did his research at Harvard University back in the 1920's, he realized that the vast majority of people were what he considered "normal." That is, they were not living with some kind of physical, mental or emotional malady. Therefore, rather than trying to base a model on what was WRONG with everyone, he tried to find one that was based on what was RIGHT with everyone. The DISC model is the result of his early work. Hopefully, we have added to that model to clarify it and keep it current, practical, helpful, useful, transferable and duplicatable.

Soon after Jeanine went through training, she began bringing other members of her team for training. One by one the staff members were trained in the use of the Personality Insights information. Because we are focused on the wellness model, and try to keep a positive, uplifting, edifying outlook on all that we teach, it was little wonder that the work Jeanine was trying to accomplish fit like a hand in a glove with the work at Personality Insights. It has been an honor to know her, to work with her, and to learn from her.

My Ph.D. is in Higher Education Administration and Counseling. Earlier in my career, I was a school principal. As an educator and as the father of four beautiful daughters, I am excited about *The Dance of Interaction*. Jeanine has done an exceptional job of giving her readers powerful insights into new ways to help children become happier and more successful. She shows teachers and parents how to find creative solutions to the difficult problems that they encounter while working with children. *The Dance of Interaction* is full of stories and ideas that give hope and help to those who love children.

This book is a huge effort on Jeanine's part. Because she is so busy and keeps such a full-time load, it has been extremely difficult for her to find the time and energy to complete this work. I want to congratulate her on staying focused to the end of this project. The reader has a rare jewel in his or her hand that can be used in many different applications. I trust you will take the time to read this work carefully and allow it to make a major difference in your life and in your relationships.

Congratulations, Jeanine! We are proud of you! We love you, respect you, and we are grateful for all you have done to help us here at Personality Insights.

Respectfully,

Dr. Robert A. Rohm, Ph.D.
President, Personality Insights, Inc.
Atlanta, Georgia

ACKNOWLEDGEMENTS

This book is not the work of one person, but the compilation of the works of many wise individuals who have allowed me to enter into their lives and who have shared of themselves so freely. At times, the power of their influence was subtle and delivered through a quiet, gentle strength. At other times, the influence was bold and straightforward, leaving one feeling like the fist of a champion fighter had struck her. Some are considered the "silent partners," having provided their influence indirectly and never having had an opportunity to know the power of their influence. To all of these individuals, I am deeply indebted.

I would like to thank Dr. Robert Rohm and his associates at Personality Insights, Inc. It is through their training and publications that my knowledge of the DISC model has evolved. These professionals have a way of presenting information about behavioral styles and relationships, so I could easily understand it and readily apply it to my everyday interactions. This knowledge has allowed me to create partnerships and opportunities I may not otherwise have had the privilege of experiencing. Their involvement in my life has been empowering and everlasting!

My sincerest thanks to the hundreds of educators and child care providers who recognized the feasibility of a book such as this. It is through their persistence, encouragement and belief in me that the courage to undertake such a feat became possible. Were it not for their support and enthusiastic interest, this book would not have been written.

Special thanks to the parents and children I have worked with over the years. Through our conversations, struggles and successes together, I grew in my understanding of the realities of parenting and what it takes to enrich the life of every child. Everyone has a story to share and once shared, it is to be respected. It is with respect and the deepest gratitude that I pass on the lessons learned from your stories and experiences.

PREFACE

The idea of writing this book was first conceived by my mentor, Janice Caputi, in 1990. At first, the thought was overwhelming and self-doubt overcame me. Since that time, I have had the privilege of working with many children - their families, educators and child care providers. Through these experiences, I have learned valuable lessons about the human spirit and behavior. I have worked diligently to share and apply this knowledge in my daily interactions with others. At the request and persistence of hundreds of individuals, *The Dance of Interaction* was written, fourteen years after its conception.

My purpose for writing this book is simple - to share some child development theory and many experiences that will empower you to become an unforgettable, positive influence in the life of every child you touch, even those whose behaviors you find disturbing, frustrating or challenging. The book is based on the belief that one of the single most important factors in a child's success is having a relationship with a supportive, competent adult. This connection is developed and maintained through a bond of unconditional acceptance, mutual respect and trust. All that we do with and for children flows from this relationship, including communicating, playing, nurturing, protecting, disciplining and teaching. As parents, educators and child care providers, our effectiveness with children lies in our understanding of and ability to create this bond. This book will offer practical suggestions for achieving this outcome, so that a child who does the "cha cha" through life does not have an adult who only knows how to "hustle." Instead, both can "waltz" their way through the journey together.

The Dance of Interaction is based on a second belief - an ounce of prevention is worth a pound of cure. Prevention makes the difference between safety and danger, order or chaos, and a child's sense of security and trust or insecurity and mistrust. It is far more effective to anticipate, plan and respond to a child's behavior, than to react to a behavior or crisis situation that ensues.

We make choices every day about how we use our time with children. When we prevent and respond, we have chosen to invest our time. As with money, time invested over the long haul produces measurable, durable gains and dividends. It is planning for the future. The dividends will include a future society of individuals with strong character and self-discipline. These individuals will be ones who become lifelong learners with a sense of community that allows them to reach beyond themselves and provide service to others. Along the journey, there will be temporary setbacks and losses. During these times, never lose sight of the prize and always celebrate the joys and wonders of childhood. The power of your influence in the lives of others cannot be measured in dollars and cents. It is measured in love.

INTRODUCTION

"There are many children with disturbing behaviors, but they are not all disturbed." Many years ago, Eleanor Lewis taught me this lesson. Her words are as true today as they were on the day she first spoke them.

These words set me on a mission to engage in studies in education and mental health on a broader scale. In particular, I was concerned about the number of children being identified with challenging behavior. I was also concerned about the adults caring for or educating children, and the demands these behaviors placed upon them. I was intrigued about the possible reasons for the changes being observed. And, most importantly, I wanted to be part of the solution to what appeared to be a growing trend.

In 1986, I began to research this trend. Using data gathered from programs and schools throughout New England, six percent of the children in programs were identified with behaviors that were described as challenging. The number one behavior was noncompliance, which means the child did not initiate an appropriate response to an adult's directions within ten to fifteen seconds of having heard it. This is what most people refer to as not listening.

By 1996, the data revealed a changing trend. The number of children identified with challenging behaviors had increased to eighteen percent. No longer was noncompliance the number one behavior of concern. Acute physical behavior had taken its place on the list of concerns for parents, educators and child care providers. Acute physical behaviors are those that present a clear and imminent danger to the child, others or property. This is what most people refer to as aggression, violence and destructiveness.

Today, the number of children with challenging behaviors has increased again. It now stands at twenty-one percent.

In the chapters that follow, you will embark on a journey that will lead you toward the solutions.

ANATOMY OF THE DANCE

According to Drs. Stanley Greenspan and T. Berry Brazelton, "We need to understand human functioning not only at the biological level, but also at its psychological, social and cultural levels. Simplistic reward and punishment approaches to feelings and behaviors tend to produce negativism and rebellion, or fear, anxiety and passivity. There are alarming increases in the number of children presenting for evaluation and treatment. And children are being put on three or four medications to deal with complicated family patterns and stress. And three fourths are not receiving the services to teach the coping skills they need."[1]

This section will examine behavior through the holistic lens suggested by Greenspan.

CHAPTER 1

IT'S ALL IN YOUR HAND

"We have no say over the hand dealt
us in life,
but we do have a lot of control
over how the hand is played..."

Roberta Andresen [2]

1

I magine with me, that we are watching a group of people playing a modified version of poker. The basic rules are as follows: Each person is dealt one card. There is no opportunity to draw a new card. There are no wild cards. The players will move around the room showing their card and viewing the cards of others. Each person will find four people to join up with in order to make a winning poker hand.

The game begins. The noise level increases as the players begin to move around the room. We hear one woman mutter, "Loser," as she looks down at her card. Other players chatter excitedly as they call out their plans to make a flush, straight or full house.

We hear a group of voices calling out to one woman, "Come here; we need you!" We see that woman beam with the joy of being wanted. Then we look around the room and observe other players slowly walking around the room expressing despair with every step.

It is easy to see differences in the approach that participants take. Some walk confidently around the room and find matches. Others are more reserved and proceed with hesitancy. In the end, some players find a group to join and feel the sense of belonging. Others wander around the room with their head down in silence, as they realize that they will never find a group to join.

Application

What does this game of poker have to do with raising and educating children? This game mirrors many of the aspects of life. It demonstrates that as we move through life, we deal with many different issues such as communicating, cooperating, dealing with losing, and dealing with difficult feelings such as rejection, loneliness and hopelessness.

As we work with children, we can easily notice that some children generally flourish in life while others seem to flounder. Some find acceptance early in life, while others wander aimlessly for years. In addition, some children belong for a while, and then something better comes along, and then they are excluded.

Perhaps the most important lesson taught in the poker illustration is that at conception, every child is dealt a card. The card represents his personality and his talents. This card is the one he must play. As he moves about his home, community and the world, he is to find people to join with in order to make a winning hand.

Reflection

When you meet children, how do you respond to their needs? Do you say, "Hey, come here! I need and love you." Or do you allow children to wander past you feeling unnoticed or being excluded? Do children leave your presence feeling confused, rejected, humiliated and alone?

Our responsibility as parents, providers and educators is not to change the card a child is dealt. Instead, our responsibility is to help him to play his card in the best way possible. This is not a gamble, but a great investment.

I have told many parents this statement, "Your child is designed as he should be. Our goal is to work together to help him to grow into his design." With that said, let's continue along our journey.

CHAPTER 2

GO TO THE PRINCIPLE

"A child went up to his teacher and said, 'Tell me
what I can become.'
The teacher looked into
his eyes and with great wisdom responded,
'You can become all that you are.'"

Author Unknown

2

O n a backpacking trip in New Hampshire, we happened upon an old foundation. The building was no longer standing, but the stonework appeared solid. I thought about how critical it is to anchor our care for children in this type of foundation - one that endures time. In teaching and parenting, we are setting the footings for each child's future. Since failure in this effort is not an option, we must build on principles.

Principles are guidelines that govern our actions. They are unchanging foundational truths that have permanent value. Principles apply to all people in all situations. They govern the process of growth and development. Principles must not be broken, because reduced effectiveness or failure may result.

Our goal is to release the potential and uniqueness of every child, so that every child can become all that he or she is. This happens in the moments of each day, as we go about our daily interactions. And as we share these times together, it is important to acknowledge that practices may change over the years, but principles will not.

Principle #1
Every interaction leaves influence.

If I asked you to raise your hand if you consider yourself a leader, would you? If leadership were to be defined as "the ability to influence," would you raise your hand then? I submit that teaching and parenting are all about influence.

According to research, every individual will influence, directly or indirectly, ten thousand people in their lifetime. Every interaction will leave a positive or negative influence. Therefore, the real question is not, "Are you a leader?" but instead, "What kind of leader will you be?" As you encounter children, will your interactions leave each child feeling positive about the situation and about himself or herself?

As Stephen Covey writes about in the book, *The Seven Habits of Highly Effective Families*, the influence we leave will either fill or deplete the emotional bank account of a person. The emotional bank account is defined as the level of trust built into the relationship. According to Covey,[3] deposits are made into this account when we:

- Show small kindnesses.
- Apologize for our shortcomings.
- Focus on the positives or strengths of others.
- Show loyalty to those not present.
- Make and keep our promises and commitments.
- Forgive others for their shortcomings.

In this country, there are children whose account is depleted. In the financial world, a depletion of funds is called bankruptcy, and so it is in the emotional world.

Emotional bankruptcy or emotional drought may be present when a child appears hardened on the outside, maintaining an "I don't care" attitude. The child may withdraw from his world, preferring to stay isolated. Whatever it looks like to us, the child is trying to survive, and he is developing coping strategies to do so. His coping strategies display themselves as challenging behavior.

There is a critical question I have asked myself time and time again as I work with children. The question is: "If this child grew up to become a neurosurgeon and I was lying on the operating room table under his care, how would I want him to remember me and the influence I had on his life?"

Principle #2
*Children need at least one adult in their life
who loves them unconditionally.*

Unconditional love says, "I love you no matter what."

As I have told many children, "You do not have to love me, but there is nothing you will ever do or say that will stop me from loving you." Every child needs the nutrients that come from this type of love.

Unfortunately, many children experience conditional love. This love says, "I love you when...or I love you if..." Conditional love sees the child for what he does rather than who he is.

When children experience unconditional acceptance, they develop trust in their environment and the people in it. This trust becomes the foundation for their relationships and learning. Instead of being squeezed into a mold and finding it challenging to know who they are and who they are meant to become, they can develop naturally. As Carolyn Kalil states, "If I am not who I thought I was, and I can't be who I was told to be, then who am I?"[4] Children need adults that empower them to do their best in all situations and support them in the pursuit of *their* dreams.

Principle #3
*There is no such thing as a "perfect,"
"good" or "bad" child.*

Each child is uniquely designed. It does not take long to realize that no two children are alike. So how do we nurture the seeds of greatness in *every* child?

Walk to your refrigerator, open it and take out an apple. Look at the apple carefully, and write down all that you see. Your eyes may focus on the color, or you may be drawn to the size, shape, stem, label or bruises.

The way you have just studied an apple is the same way many parents and professionals study children. They see what is on the outside and then move to judgment about their potential. Children are judged by the color of their skin, their size, shape, gender or label. "What can you expect?

He's got Attention Deficit Disorder with Hyperactivity." "He'll never play professional basketball, because he's too short." Some adults only see what is wrong with, or the weakness of the child and invest their time and energy into correcting this problem, so the child becomes "perfect" or "good." They attach labels that justify the problem in some way. The question becomes: Why do we see variation or differences as being "less than?" We must remain open to differences and understand that strength comes from diversity.

Now take a sharp paring knife and slice the apple you have studied across its mid-section. You must slice it from side to side, not stem to bottom. After you have sliced it, open up the apple to reveal the embedded seeds. Pick up one seed. Observe it carefully, and write down what you believe to be the potential of that one seed. How many apples are present under the protective sheath? Can you tell? The truth is we cannot determine the fruits to be produced by looking at the seed.

As with this apple, children have seeds of potential buried deep within them. Those seeds were planted at the point of conception. By looking at each child, we cannot determine the potential of those seeds yet to be fulfilled. All we know is that they are there, and we can influence whether they remain dormant or blossom to their full potential by our daily interactions.

Next, pick up one half of the apple you have sliced. You will notice that the seeds are housed in a hardened core. It provides a shelter for what is vulnerable and precious, and so it is with children. Children rely on adults for protection. As Marian Marion stated, "Adults and children are engaged in the dance of interaction. Each influences the other in any interaction. The adults understand their role in the dance, or in the guidance system. They realize that children have an important part in any interaction, but they know that adults always have greater responsibility."[5]

Finally, as you look at the half of the apple, you will notice that the core creates a star shape. Every child can develop into the "star" that houses the seeds, while you reap the fruits of your labor. When we stop looking at all that is wrong and begin focusing on all that is right, the seeds for a better tomorrow will be planted.

Principle #4

Our emotions and thoughts precede our actions. Our actions repeated over time develop into habits. Our habits determine our character, and character determines success.

If this principle is true, and it is, then children who spend much of their time in an environment that encourages positive emotions and thoughts will tend to have more positive behaviors. This means that we must consider what creates this type of environment. It also means we must give up the myth of the "Band-Aid approach" to dealing with behavior.

Joshua

Joshua has just bitten his sister, Samantha. His mother sees the behavior as biting, and her goal is to "stop it, and stop it NOW!" Joshua's mother says, "Go to your room until I'm ready to deal with you!"

Sending Joshua to his room is like putting a Band-Aid on the behavior. It may stop the behavior temporarily, but it has not stopped the behavior forever. The behavior is not the problem but a symptom of the problem.

The problem is found in Joshua's emotions and thoughts. So what might he be feeling or thinking that could lead him to bite his sister? Biting may be the result of feeling frustrated or angry. Biting may be the result of a need for sensory stimulation to the mouth. Biting may be a way to communicate if Joshua has delayed speech and language. Biting may be Joshua's way to gain attention or get a toy. There are many emotions and thoughts that could lead to biting behavior.

Let's assume that Joshua is using the biting behavior to express anger. Is sending him to his room helping him to manage his anger, or will he need a caring adult to teach him the skills of anger management? How long will it take to teach the skills of anger management? Will it take a lot longer than this mom's current expectation of NOW?

In order to create a new habit, we must unlearn the old and relearn the new. To help a child learn a new habit requires time and teaching on the part of the adult and repeated practice on the part of the child. We can tell Joshua, "It's OK to be angry. When you are angry, you may not bite, but you may count to five or take five deep breaths." Then we must be willing to model and practice these new skills with Joshua.

Principle #5
Behavior is a result of our choices, not our situation.

As Victor Frankl stated many years ago, "Between what happens and how we respond to it, is the freedom or power to choose."

In the previous situation, Joshua was experiencing anger. Before he bit Samantha, he could have paused to consider what his options were in that situation. He might have thought, "I could bite her, but that would get me into trouble." Or he might have thought, "I'll go play with somebody else." Joshua had a choice.

After the emotion and between the thoughts and actions, is the *power of the pause*. This is the point of choice and decision. In order for children to take advantage of this pause, they must possess impulse control. An impulse is defined as an emotion bursting into action. Controlling impulses requires children to stop and think before they act. Many children lag behind developmentally in this area.

Today, more and more children are identified with Attention Deficit Disorder with Hyperactivity. One of the hallmark characteristics of this label is a lack of impulse control. Although ADHD is a valid diagnosis, could the increasing number of children being diagnosed be a reflection of their culture?

As food for thought, there may be significant adults in the lives of these children that model this impulsivity. During my childhood, credit cards, debit cards and ATM machines did not exist. My parents saved for what they needed to buy. This supported the development of delayed gratification. Today, with access to the above conveniences, impulse buying has become a problem. Parents are not only buying what they need on credit, but what they do not need. Children watch their parents buying whatever they want, whenever they want it, by taking out a small piece of plastic. Not understanding the financial obligations behind these conveniences, children perceive immediate gratification as normal and expected behavior.

The normal eating behavior of today's families also adds to the expectation of immediate gratification. During my childhood, we did not have microwave ovens and fast-food restaurants to the degree they are available today. Coffee was perked in a percolator pot, and meals were prepared from scratch, with fresh ingredients. This preparation took much longer than popping a hot dog in the microwave for 30 seconds or driving by McDonald's on the way home from activities. Today, the average family meal consists of driving up to a speaker and menu board and ordering items. This reinforces an attitude of getting things NOW. Moreover, the interaction between the parent and the fast-food worker models the rushed climate of our day. Children hear the impatient voice over the intercom demanding, "Six pieces or eight pieces? What kind of sauce? Small, medium or large fries?" These everyday experiences add to the expectation of immediate gratification.

Other examples of modern conveniences that add to the expectation of immediate gratification are computers, fax machines, DVD players and video games. In many homes today, children and adults are sitting in separate rooms; each one is connected to some type of technology or media. One may be on the laptop catching up on work, while another one is playing video games. Yet another is text messaging on a cell phone. All of this technology gives a child a sense that he should have things instantly.

Our society is moving further and further away from the under-standing of the need to wait patiently. Is it any wonder why we have so many children who lack impulse control?

Principle #6
The privileges you earn are in direct proportion to the amount of responsibility you accept.

There are parents who have become the entertainment agents for their children. As soon as Sarah says, "I want to…" or "Get me…" her parents run to meet the demand. After all, this keeps her happy and that is important.

What this really does is let Sarah believe that everything she wants is owed to her and owed immediately. Sarah begins to see everything as a right. Instead, we must get back to teaching our children that there are rights, such as the right to safety, and there are privileges, such as the privilege of getting a toy or staying up late. Rights are given, and privileges are earned.

All children should have responsibilities that are appropriate for their age. For example, toddlers can put their dirty clothes into the laundry basket and help clean their room, while preschoolers can help set the table, prepare meals and sort silverware when it comes out of the dishwasher, as well as sort laundry and clean their room. School-age children can be responsible for doing their homework, doing the laundry or dishes, as well as cleaning their room. And, the acceptance of these responsibilities must always precede privileges earned.

Principle #7
It is not nurture versus nature, but nurture and nature.

Depending on the theory used for understanding behavior, some will advocate that the child acts as he does because that is who he is by genetics. This is the nature theory. It supports the belief that children have particular ways of taking in and understanding sensations from their world, and organizing and planning actions. Others take the position that it is the experiences and interactions we provide for the child that influences the behavior and by changing variables in the environment, the behavior changes. This is the nurture theory. These two schools of thought led to what was known as the "nurture versus nature" debate in the field of psychology.

Modern research has allowed us to merge the two schools of thought into what is referred to as the "Developmental Duet," according to Drs. Greenspan and Brazelton.[6] We now see that the two work together. The experiences and interactions of a child can unlock the child's nature and unseen potential.

Principle #8
You can ignore some behaviors, but you cannot ignore the need behind the behavior.

All behavior serves a purpose. Behavior can be a way to communicate an unmet need, express emotions or thoughts, or keep a child safe. Rudolf Dreikurs, an expert in the area of classroom behavior, believes there are four mistaken goals that precede bad behavior. The child is seeking attention, gaining power, getting revenge or working to get another person to believe he is inadequate. For example: Melissa is a child who tries to get attention by whining. Adults can ignore the whining behavior, but the need for attention is still present. And, that need must be met. Therefore, Melissa needs to be taught other ways to gain attention but not at the time she is whining. She needs to be told, "I can see that you want my attention. Attention is not a bad thing, but when you want it, please ask for a hug or for my attention."

Principle #9
When we ignore children's whispers of behavior, we force them to shout.

Brian

Brian is five years old and attends a child care program with nineteen other children in his class. I am called to his classroom one morning. Upon arrival, I notice that Brian is the only child in the room with Mrs. Clark, his teacher. He is sitting at a table, with his coat on, crying. Mrs. Clark angrily barks, "You deal with him!"

Since I have never met Brian before, I approach him and introduce myself. "Hi, Brian, I know you don't know me, but my name is Jeanine. It's nice to meet you. I'll be back to talk with you in a few minutes. Right now, I am going to speak to Mrs. Clark." He nods his head and stops crying.

I pull Mrs. Clark to the side and ask her a few questions. "What happened, and why is he inside?" She tells me that he threw sand in her face while the class was outside playing. I then ask her to recount his day since his arrival to now, which was 11:30 in the morning.

She states that Brian arrived at 7:30 that morning. When he entered, he said, "I'm mad!" This comment is a whisper of behavior that was ignored. Instead of acknowledging and validating his emotion, he was instructed to hang up his backpack and wash his hands for breakfast. Brian washed his hands and came to the breakfast table. He proceeded to fill his bowl with cereal and then dumped it on the floor. Mrs. Clark demanded that he pick the KIX up, and while he was doing so, he was to count the number of individual pieces he dumped. Brian picked them up but did not count the pieces. He then poured milk onto the cereal and dumped the bowl to the floor once again. All of these behaviors are whispers of behavior that are getting louder in hopes that his teacher will help him with his anger.

The morning continued with one incident after another until Brian was unable to contain his building emotions, and he threw sand into his teacher's face. This was his shout. At this point, Mrs. Clark could not contain her emotions and brought Brian inside and sought help.

After processing the situation with Mrs. Clark, I ask her to approach Brian in a supportive manner, so he will remain calm while we work to resolve the situation. I encourage her to walk over to where he is sitting and sit in a chair about three to five feet from him. I coach her to say, "Brian, I know you're mad. I know this, because when you came to school this morning, you told me that you were mad. Then, you dumped your cereal on the floor, and now, you have thrown sand in my eyes. What can we do to make this day better for both of us?"

Mrs. Clark then walks over to Brian and leans over the table, putting her face approximately one foot from Brian's face. She states, "Brian, I know you're mad. Why are you mad?"

At this point, Brian leans over the table and with great emphasis says, "Because I'm sitting here with my coat on, and I'm sweating!"

This had nothing to do with Brian's anger. In working with him myself, I found out that his mother promised to volunteer at his school that day. However, before he left for school, she decided not to volunteer and sent him off by himself. That is why he entered his classroom stating, "I'm mad." And, the ensuing behaviors could have been stopped or minimized by listening to his words (the whispers), and not waiting for the negative actions to express his anger (the shouts).

Principle #10
Behavior is not acceptable or unacceptable.

Behaviors are determined acceptable and appropriate depending on the environment and situation. What serves a child well in one environment may not in another. When my daughter, Erin, was small, I taught her, "Never spit. Spitting is a gross and disgusting behavior, and it spreads lots of germs." Later, I brought her to the dentist. Within the first five minutes of this appointment, the dentist told Erin to spit. She looked at me and began to cry. I realized that I had made a mistake. I needed to have included appropriate times to spit when I was teaching about spitting. For example, I could have said, "Spitting is OK in the dentist's office and when you brush your teeth."

When my daughter was a teenager, we encountered another example of principle # 10. Erin has the gift of gab. This behavior served her well in cheerleading, coaching cheerleading teams and being a part-time waitress. Nevertheless, it was a hindrance during silent reading at school.

These two examples from Erin's life show that the same behavior can be helpful at times and unacceptable at times. Therefore, the idea that behavior is always acceptable or unacceptable does not exist. Instead children must learn to control their emotions and behaviors in ways that are appropriate to the situation and environment they are in at the time.

In closing, it is important to acknowledge that we have choices. The secret to our success as educators, providers or parents is to align our behavior and practices with principles.

CHAPTER 3

PIECES OF THE PUZZLE

"There's been something I've been holding back on.
I just wanted to express to you how special you are to
our family.
It's not what you do, and it's not what you've done.
It's who you are as a person.
I love you and just wanted you to know
that I love you."

Gene Bedley [7]

3

Whn a child's behavior presents a challenge, our first reaction is to see what we can do to stop it quickly. Rarely, will we take the time to find out why the child did it. This search for the "quick fix" becomes obvious when parents and educators ask questions that begin with "What do I do when…"

- What do I do when Alex hits his brother?
- What do I do when Mikayla is rude?
- What do I do when Joel doesn't listen to anything I say?
- What do I do when Brooke does not stay in her own bed?
- What do I do when Christopher has a tantrum?
- What do I do when Madison will not clean up her room?

This is known as the cookbook approach to behavior. The problem with this approach is that the ingredients are not the same from child to child. There are no "quick-fix" recipes.

Think for a moment. You enter the doctor's office with symptoms of fatigue, a headache and difficulty concentrating. The doctor tells you to rest for a couple of days and take two aspirin every four hours for headaches. He suggests that you are probably overworked and stressed out. However, after following the doctor's orders, the symptoms do not subside. A full examination reveals you have a thyroid condition. Obviously, the treatment for stress and hypothyroidism are very different. In-depth assessment and accurate identification of the cause are needed to determine the most effective treatment. This is also true with behavior.

Elizabeth

Quite a few years ago, I had the opportunity to meet a little girl named Elizabeth. Elizabeth was four years old at the time and living in a rural community with her grandfather. Every morning at nine o'clock, Elizabeth would enter the classroom with a smile on her face. She was brought to school each morning by her grandfather. There was a quick goodbye, and she was off to play with her friends.

By 10:30 each morning, Elizabeth's behaviors began to change. She refused to join her friends at the morning circle. Instead, she would hit them, throw toys at them, kick her teachers and scream. When her teacher gave directions to the class to get their coats and line up, Elizabeth would not respond. In fact, she would run and hide under the teacher's desk. During lunch, Elizabeth would cry and refuse to eat.

At 12:30, Elizabeth was picked up at school by her grandfather and reluctantly returned to her home. If we were to make some assumptions about Elizabeth's behaviors, we might think she did not like being in a large group or having to go outside. We might hypothesize that she was getting tired and children who are tired do not play and socialize well with their peers. We might assume that Elizabeth does not adjust to changes and transitions easily, or that the morning meeting was boring and not meaningful for Elizabeth. There are many assumptions we might reach.

Depending on the assumption, we could then plan strategies that we believe would be helpful to Elizabeth. For example, when the assumption is that the morning meeting is boring and not meaningful to Elizabeth, we could add activities to the meeting that would be of interest to her. A second strategy might be to excuse her from the morning meeting and ask her to help a teacher with an errand. If, however, we choose the assumption that Elizabeth is tired and children who are tired do not play and socialize well with their peers, the strategy might be to talk to her grandfather about her sleep habits and routines. We could also offer her a soft, cozy, private space to rest. In both of these scenarios, we are working with Elizabeth's behaviors, not based on facts, but based on our assumptions.

The facts of this story are that Elizabeth does not want to go back home with her grandfather. Her mother gave birth to her at the age of thirteen. Elizabeth was removed from her mother's care at birth, and custody was awarded to her maternal grandfather. Her mother is diagnosed with Bipolar Disorder. Elizabeth does not know her mother. Her grandfather lives with his girlfriend who is diagnosed with schizophrenia. In the home, there are issues with abuse. Elizabeth finds her home a place where her safety is compromised. Her behaviors serve to communicate this message.

With the facts in hand, how does this information alter our thoughts about effective strategies? Do we still think that changing the activities at morning meeting will be beneficial?

All behavior serves a purpose. Even if the child cannot communicate the purpose or meaning, this does not negate the fact that there is a reason. In understanding the meaning of the behaviors, a greater level of empathy toward the child emerges. We are then in a position to respond with sensitivity to the behavior, instead of reacting from our own assumptions and emotions.

There is a framework that we can apply to look at the whole child and the context of the child's behavior. This framework will help us discover the meaning and possible explanation for the behavior. It answers the question, "Why does she do that?" The awareness we gather by applying this framework increases the likelihood of structuring the environment to better "fit" the child's characteristics. By adjusting this fit, we become more effective and efficient in our responses.

I will begin to introduce you to the seven - piece framework for evaluating a child's problem behavior by explaining the need to gain as much information as you can about the child. It is important to paint a picture of this child. Answer questions such as,

What are his physical characteristics? (hair color, height, etc.)

What does he like to do?

In what situations does he show his strengths and experience success?

What situations challenge or frustrate him?

What goes on in his home?

Once the picture is complete, it is time for you to focus on those traits that are challenging for this child, other children or you. Describe what he does in specific terms. For example, I got a call from a teacher that was having trouble with a student named Matthew. Matthew was taking toys from his classmates without asking permission. I knew that all behaviors serve a purpose; therefore, there was a reason behind this behavior. My job is to find the reason. Finding the reason is much like uncovering hidden clues. Actually, the framework I use is a seven-piece puzzle. Each piece of the puzzle looks at one area that could offer a possible explanation. The puzzle is only complete when all seven areas have been fully explored. Here are the seven pieces of the puzzle:

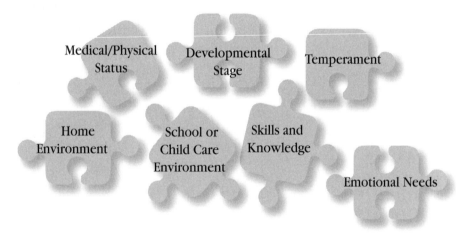

As you use this framework to explore a behavior, begin with the first piece of the puzzle. Move through all the pieces looking for clues until you feel you have found the best "fit" between your picture of the child and the possible explanations. It is possible to have more than one explanation or influence. Do not rush your search for clues. Set your sights on the "big picture."

In this next section, I will explain each of the seven pieces of the diagnosis framework and give one or more examples.

The truth of the situation was that Michael did listen to some things his mother had to say, but not everything. When it comes to responding to directions, children the age of Michael are considered within the "normal range" when they respond sixty percent of the time. This means that out of every ten directions given to him, he will initiate a response six out of the ten times. This Michael did. However, his mother was frustrated by the other forty percent, because her expectation was immediate obedience to her every command.

Jennifer

Jennifer was an eight-year-old child who had temper tantrums at least five times a day. The tantrums consisted of slamming doors, yelling, and stomping her feet. Developmentally, temper tantrums are to by the fourth birthday; otherwise, this form of behavior may become Jennifer's dominant style of manipulating others to do what she wants of or to get what she wants. This behavior does not fall within the normal range" for a child of eight years.

TEMPERAMENT

The third puzzle piece is Temperament.

How can I tell if the behavior is explained by temperament?

You have talked with the child's parents and have learned that the trait has been consistent since birth.

You have read about this in books or articles on temperament and know that it is a part of a particular temperament type or blend.

This behavior cannot be explained by the developmental stage alone.

You have studied the child through observation and this trait is predictable in his pattern of behavior.

MEDICAL/PHYSICAL STATUS

The first puzzle piece is the Medical/Physical Status.

How can I tell if a behavior is explained by a child's medical or physical status?

- Check the most recent physical examination report, within one year of the date, for signs of physical concerns.

- Check to see if she is on any medications or has been in the recent past, such as asthma medication, cough syrup, Ritalin, etc.

- Make sure the child's hearing and vision is within "normal" limits.

- Ask about the child's sleep and eating habits. Does she get restful sleep? Does she get a full night's sleep? Is she getting a balanced diet?

- Ask if there is a history of disabilities or disorders in the family, such as Attention Deficit Disorder with Hyperactivity, Depression, Dyslexia, Anxiety, Sensory Integration Dysfunction, etc.

- Check the child's dental health records.

Christopher

Christopher was a five-year-old child who attended a kindergarten program. I was asked to come into the classroom to observe Christopher, because the teacher said, "He's spacey!" In clarifying what that meant, she stated that she thought he had Attention Deficit Disorder.

I went to the classroom and observed Christopher on more than one occasion. It was true that there were periods of time throughout the day that Christopher was focused on his work and other times he was not. In reviewing the data gathered during these observations, there appeared to be a pattern that indicated a medical concern. From 8:30 to 11:00 a.m., Christopher was paying attention. As the morning wore on, his attention began to drift off. Lunch came and after lunch, Christopher was focused again. By 2:30, his attention was drifting again.

In reviewing the family medical history, there was a strong history of diabetes. Christopher was referred to his primary care physician and diagnosed with diabetes. The recommended treatment for his diabetic condition was very different then what might have been recommended for ADD.

Amy

Amy was a three-year-old who attended a family child care home with five children close to her age. The behavior that was concerning to the provider was biting. Amy had been biting since she was eighteen months old. The provider stated that she had tried everything and nothing worked. The call for help was quite urgent.

I observed Amy playing with the children in this home. The first thing I noticed was that Amy walked over three times and asked for a drink from the provider's coffee cup. I thought it was rather unusual for a child of her age to like coffee and for her to continue to ask for sips. Next, Amy was playing in a dramatic play area and began putting toys into her mouth. Again, it occurred to me that this is an infant behavior and quite unusual for a preschooler. The third incident involved Amy and one other child sitting with me, reading a story. Amy leaned toward the other child and bit her arm. This appeared to come out of the blue. Once she bit her, she smiled. Again, this was not typical of biting behavior in the preschool-age group.

I asked the provider if this was the biting pattern that she had been seeing. She said, "Yes."

Then I asked, "Do you do musical instruments with the children?" Again she gave an affirmative answer. "What is Amy's favorite instrument?"

"A whistle."

"Do you ever do bubble blowing with the children?"

"Yes, but only when we go outside, because they ruin the rug. Blowing bubbles is Amy's favorite thing to do."

I then gave the teacher the following instructions: Every day sure that Amy has access to a sippy cup of water. When she needs she can get the cup and sip. Then, put the whistle in her pocket, she needs to blow, it's there. Make sure she has a straw for her snack and lunch.

When the provider questioned my instructions, I told h suspicion was that Amy needed increased stimulation to her mou got the stimulation through biting, drinking, blowing and putti her mouth. After 4 days, I received a call from Amy's provider, elated because the biting had stopped.

What was being treated as a developmental behav a concern with sensory integration. Amy was referred to a therapist for an evaluation and a sensory diet was designed.

DEVELOPMENTAL STAGE

The second puzzle piece is Developmental Stag

How can I tell if the behavior is explained by developmental stage?

- Consult child development books to see if this the child's age.

- Note if you have seen other children the sam

- Consider your behavior at the same age.

Michael

Michael was a four-year-old child w by his behavior. She told me, "He doesn't lis hear me? Nothing. He listens to nothing! How

Pam

Pam was a four-year-old child. Her teacher was getting greatly annoyed with Pam's frequent desire to tell long or outrageous stories. I was called to the class to observe Pam. Shortly after I arrived in the classroom, Pam walked up to the teacher and said with great enthusiasm, "Can I tell you a story?"

The teacher said, "Yes."

Pam said, "Really?"

"Yes, Pam."

Pam continued, "Well ok. My dad wears my mom's nightgown."

Making sure she understood the message, the teacher asked, "Did you just tell me that your dad wears your mom's nightgown?" Pam beamed with a smile from ear to ear and shook her head *yes*. The teacher asked her what she thought of her dad.

Pam flipped her hands forward and said, "I think he's silly." The teacher reflected back that her dad wearing her mom's nightgown was silly. Again Pam smiled and said, "Yeah, 'cuz watch what he does." She proceeded to dance in a circle, while alternately pointing her fingers into the air.

The teacher, not knowing what to say, asked, "What does your mom think of your dad dancing in her nightgown?"

Pam took a deep breath, smiled one more time and said, "Oh, she just tells him he's a stupid dipshit."

After observing Pam, I learned that, in addition to storytelling, Pam had other obvious personality traits that signaled that she was a high "I" personality style. The "I" temperament is one of four personality styles in the DISC Model of Human Behavior. Understanding temperaments provides keys to being effective with children and also allows adults to enjoy children to the greatest extent. In-depth information about temperaments is given in a later chapter.

I explained to Pam's teacher that storytelling is a natural behavior in high "I" children. Then I coached the teacher by explaining better ways to interact with Pam, including how to provide appropriate times for storytelling, so that Pam and the teacher would have a more positive relationship.

HOME ENVIRONMENT

The next puzzle piece is called Home Environment.

How can I tell if a child's behavior is explained by something in the home environment?

- The behavior has changed suddenly, and there are difficulties that the child is experiencing at home, such as the birth of a sibling, separation or divorce, substance abuse, domestic violence, etc.

- There are conflicting styles in parenting.

- There is a conflict between different parts of the child's world. The home and school have different values, beliefs, practices, culture and philosophies about children.

- Birth order issues are present. [8]

Peter

Peter was a five-year-old child who lived with his mother. One day, Peter picked up a cast-iron cash register and threw it through a second story, plate-glass window. This was Peter's way of letting his teachers know that he was angry.

As I was working with Peter, his mom arrived and said, "What are you doing to my son?"

I responded, "Talking with him."

She told him to stand up and get his coat, because they were leaving.

"You do not have to listen to her. She's not your mother."

Later that day, I called the mom on the phone to follow up on this incident. The mother invited me to the home to talk things through. While on this visit, Peter walked over to a console stereo in the living room and pulled out a plastic bag with white powder, a tourniquet and a syringe. He carried the items to the other side of the room, sat on the couch and wrapped the tourniquet around his arm. Peter pretended to give himself an injection with the syringe that he filled with the powder. While this was happening, his mom was unaware of his activities, because she could not see him from where she sat.

It appeared that Peter was angry for some valid reasons. He was growing up in a home of a heroin addict. Moreover, he was frequently left alone while his mother was out. She said, "He's never left alone. The neighbor downstairs can hear him and leaves her door unlocked if he needs help."

Peter's behaviors were influenced by parental neglect.

"It is a wise father that knows his own child."
William Shakespeare

School or Child Care Environment

The next puzzle piece is School or Child Care Environment.

How can I tell if a child's behavior is explained by something in the classroom or child care environment?

- The medical or physical status, developmental stage, temperament or home environment does not explain the behavior.
- Many in the group or class have the same behavior.
- When the environment changes, the behavior changes.

Brandon

Brandon is a three-year-old child. The teacher referred him to me because of his activity level in the classroom. Brandon runs from one learning center to another and seems to enjoy wrestling with his peers.

When I looked at the layout of the environment, there was a large, open space in the middle of the room. This open space encouraged high activity levels and rough and tumble play. We redesigned the layout, and Brandon's activity level dropped.

Skills and Knowledge

The sixth puzzle piece is Skills and Knowledge.

How can I tell if a child's behavior is explained by a lack of skills or knowledge?

- The medical or physical status, developmental stage, temperament, home environment or school environment do not explain the behavior.
- The child is in a new and unfamiliar place or situation.
- The child is learning a new skill.

Andrew

Andrew was a nine-year-old child. One day, Andrew yelled at his mother, "I hate you!"

Andrew's father reacted by yelling back, "You go to your room. Do not ever talk back to your mother."

Talking back is a difficult behavior for parents. However, the skill the child lacks is assertiveness. In talking back, the child uses an aggressive tone of voice or choice of words that we find offensive, and that is what we object to. In assertiveness, the child uses his words in a respectful manner. What I say to children is, "I think it's great you can use your words to tell me how you feel. But when you do, please make sure you talk to me in a respectful way."

EMOTIONAL NEEDS

The seventh puzzle piece is Emotional Needs.

How can I tell if a child's behavior is an attempt to satisfy an unmet emotional need?

All of the following are present:

- The behavior is not appropriate for a child of his age.
- The behavior is persistent. It has a driven quality. The child has to do it, and the child brings intensity to the behavior that is noticeable to the adult.
- The behavior, even when stopped and channeled, later reoccurs.
- The usual ways of handling and helping children with this behavior do not seem to work.

Mark

Mark is a young child who was having temper tantrums every day. His tantrums would last up to four hours at a time. Despite intervention, the tantrum behavior continued for two years.

After introducing myself to Mark's mother, she said, "I know what you do. You are not going to play head games with my kid. In fact, don't talk to me about loving him, because I do not even like him. If there was an electrical storm tonight, I would tie him to a tree and hope he got electrocuted."

While working with Mark, it was clear that his mom had some emotional needs that had not been met. (As a parent, it is difficult to provide to your children what you do not have yourself.) It appeared that Mark's mom was not empathic toward her son because she had not consistently experienced empathy in her own life. It appeared that she did not understand unconditional love, because her childhood and adult relationships were based in criticism and harsh correction of her mistakes. Therefore, our conclusion was to model empathic responses and unconditional love, so that she could see them in action. In addition, it seemed important to highlight her strengths and what she brought to her relationship with Mark. And through these efforts, her self-concept changed and her parenting skills increased. At the end of three years, Mark's mom said, "I don't know how to thank you. All I can tell you is that I not only like him, but I love him." (And it is essential to add, she not only liked herself but she loved who she had become as a person and mother.)

OVERVIEW OF THE PIECES OF THE PUZZLE[9]

Can this pattern of behavior be explained by the medical status?

YES

When the cause is determined to be a congenital health or organic condition, then the child's ability to change the behavior may be limited. The majority of the accommodation will need to come from the environment rather than the child.

Refer this child for medical evaluation with a primary care physician or specialist.

NO

Can the behavior be explained by the child's developmental stage?

YES

The actions are to be taken in the following order:

Remember that most children do this and this child may need to do it, too. The behavior will end as the child matures. **TRY TO RELAX.**

Understand this behavior is developmentally significant and serves a purpose for the child. Stay focused on what the child is achieving through this behavior.

Channel the behavior to certain places at certain times or find alternatives ways for the child to get the purpose met.

Stop the behavior when it becomes a danger or disruptive. However, be aware that the behavior will occur again.

NO

Next Page

57

Is the behavior explained by an individual difference or temperament? — YES →

Adapt your expectations and your interactions with the child.

Whenever possible, offer options that allow for and appreciate the uniqueness of this child. **Create** a "goodness of fit" through **individualization.**

NO ↓

Can the behavior be explained by the environment? — YES →

Then, **change the environment.**

When possible, change and adapt the expectations. Maintain a non-judgmental attitude. The child may have little or no control over the situation.

If the child is unsafe, seek consultation from Protective Services.

NO ↓

Can the behavior be explained by a need for new skills or knowledge? — YES →

Teach the skills. Focusing on negative behaviors without teaching alternative skills is counterproductive.

Explain reasons to children. This helps them understand why and how to make better choices.

Use a child's mistakes to teach. Mistakes are opportunities to learn when treated as such.

ROLE MODEL what is being taught and allow opportunities for the child to practice.

NO ↓

Next Page

Can this behavior be explained by attempts to meet emotional needs?

YES

Figure out what need this child is trying to meet through this behavior.

Brainstorm more appropriate ways to get this need met. *Ignoring behavior may only create a stronger drive to get this need satisfied.* Respond to the child with loving actions and words, through giving positive reinforcement and support. Try to avoid withholding and punishment.

Meet the child's needs in a firm but gentle way. **Stop the behavior when the child is hurting himself, others or destroying property.**

Get additional support for yourself, the child or others, when necessary.

UNDERSTANDING YOUR DANCE PARTNER

A child is born, and the dance of interaction begins. In this journey called life, we begin by understanding ourselves and grow to understand how we interact with others. Healthy relationships are based on understanding "me" and respecting "we."

This section will provide a glimpse into this journey.

CHAPTER 4

NURTURING THE YOUNG, THE RESTLESS, THE BOLD AND THE BEAUTIFUL

*"Educating the mind, without educating the heart is
no education at all."*

Aristotle

4

From my experience of working with hundreds of parents over the years and raising three children, there appear to be two common threads that bind parents together in their role. The first is that the majority have expressed their desire to do what is in the best interest of their children, and want others to do the same. The second is that parents want their children to have a quality of life that is equal to or better than the one they are living. This tells me that most parents deeply love their children and have dreams for their future.

There have been studies done of children who come from loving homes. The children in the studies range in age from four to ten years. These children have been asked, "Do your parents love you?"

The hope was that a resounding chorus of children would respond, "Of course my parents love me." But, this was not the case.

The greatest number of children answered, "I think they do," or "I hope they do." Others said, "I don't know." All of these responses leave room for uncertainty in the mind of the child. A small percentage said, "I don't care if they do," or "They don't love me." Those that knew without a shadow of a doubt that they were loved represented the minority.

So how do we start out as parents that deeply love our children and end up with children who question that love or do not feel loved at all? The answer is quite simple. There is a difference between being loved and feeling loved.

A valuable resource about expressing love is the book, *The Five Love Languages of Children* by Gary Chapman and Ross Campbell. These two men have found that there are several different love languages in the world, and they teach the reader that we must become "multilingual" in expressing love.[10] Their work has identified that every child and adult has a particular way of knowing that he or she is loved and cared for by others *and* a particular way of letting others know that he or she loves and cares for them. Often, in the dance of interaction, we do not stop to think that our personal preferences for giving love may not be what the other person needs from us. As a result, the individual, whether child or adult may feel unloved by us, because we are communicating in a style they do not understand. Let's look more closely at these languages of love.

THE FIVE LOVE LANGUAGES

TOUCH

There are five different love languages. The first one is physical touch.[11] Children, who understand the emotional connection with significant adults in their life through touch, may hug and kiss, cuddle, sit in your lap, engage in rough and tumble play or wrestling, ask for their back or shoulders to be rubbed or scratched, their hair to be brushed, or want to hold your hand. In contrast, there are children who prefer not to be touched unless they initiate the contact. These children have a three to five foot distance around them and do not want others entering into that imaginary space unless permission has been granted to do so.

Kyle

The dance of interaction gets out of sync when we, as adults, have the language of physical touch and the child does not or vice versa. For example, Kyle was a child who craved touch. Kyle would touch his classmates by giving them bear hugs as they entered the classroom - at times knocking them to the ground.   While at morning meeting, Kyle would hug the child next to him or pat the child on the shoulder or back. Unfortunately, his teacher, would make physical contact with her students only on rare occasions. Her rule was, "Keep your hands to yourself!" Whenever Kyle touched another child, she stated the rule. Kyle and his teacher were not in step.

The rule would have been more accurately stated as "Keep your hands to yourself until the other person says you can touch them." This implies that children must ask before touching and the consent is based on our respect for others. There are many positive behaviors that get eliminated when the rule is "Keep your hands to yourself." Have you ever tried to greet someone by shaking hands while keeping your hands to yourself? Have you ever hugged someone without using your hands? How helpful is a pat on the back or a high five without hands? Touch is vital to the emotional well-being of children, and their emotional well-being is the foundation to social and intellectual growth.

According to Virginia Satir, children and adults need a minimum of twelve healing touches per day to maintain their emotional health. Children in multi-stressed environments may need more. Adults who do not have touch as their love language may be stretched beyond their comfort zone by children with high touch needs. One way to develop a comfort level with touch is to begin each day with twelve pennies in your left pocket. Every time touch is used to nurture a child who needs touch in his life, transfer one penny to your right pocket. The goal is to move all twelve pennies to the right pocket before the end of the day.

AFFIRMATION

The second language of love is affirmation.[12] A child may say, "I love you, Dad," over and over again, or use praise often, "You're the best mom in the whole world. I'm going to marry you!" Children who prefer affirmation may ask, "Am I being good? Will I get a sticker today?" Note that individuals who understand the emotional connection through affirmation tend to verbally celebrate the efforts and accomplishments of themselves and others. For example, "You are so good at what you do."

We tend to do for others what we would want them to do for us. So children who are affirming to others, need affirmation. However, as with touch, there are some children that do not offer affirmation or seek it.

Michael

An example of a student having the affirmation love language and his teacher having a different love language is illustrated in the following situation.

Michael ran out of the classroom and was running toward the road to go home. An adult stopped him as he was climbing the school-yard fence and returned him to the classroom. Upon his return, he was taken to an area to cool off. His teacher, Mrs. Corwin, gently spoke with Michael and then played a game with him. Her method of calming him down was textbook perfect.

Once Michael was finished with his game, he walked to the other side of the room and said to the other teacher, Miss Davis, "Your hair looks nice today." Then he walked away and joined some children at the art center.

Miss Davis reacted by looking at me in confusion and then asking, "Why did he come up to me and say something about my hair?"

"He was trying to reconnect with you. He was trying to show you love."

I could easily see the differences in the love language styles for Miss Davis and Michael. I realized that this was a missed opportunity, because Michael was communicating love through affirmation, and Miss Davis communicated love through service. All Michael was trying to do was to reconnect with her and ensure her unconditional love for him. The incident that led to him running from the classroom involved Miss Davis, and he was delivering a message to her that said, "I still love you. Do you still love me?" but it sounded like, "Your hair looks nice today."

Mark

We will now revisit Mark, the little boy with the unmet needs in the previous chapter. Mark is a child who seeks and communicates through affirmation. I knew that there would be a great likelihood that he would move toward emotional drought without affirmation. So I instructed his teacher to tell him every day, "Mark, you're my hero! We're glad you're here. This class would not be the same without you." This was welcome affirmation for a child who probably was not going to receive much in his home. It did not matter that five minutes after entering the classroom he was involved in a full-blown tantrum. The class was not the same without him. On Fridays, Mark would leave hearing these words, "I know sometimes it is hard being a kid and life's not fair, but we'll be waiting for you and your smile on Monday." Through these types of interactions, Mark was being loved and feeling loved.

GIFTS

The third language of love is gifts.[13] There are individuals who love to give and receive gifts. It seems that they enjoy the giving more than the receiving. A child with this style may walk up to you holding a picture and say, "I made this for you." Or maybe it's not a picture at all, but a rock she found, weeds...I mean flowers, she picked, or a worm.

Children who have gifts as their love language may ask, "Did you get me anything?" or "What did you buy me?" These children remember special occasions and make or buy cards or gifts for these occasions.

Anthony

Anthony was playing outside with his class. He bent over, picked up a rock and put it into his pocket. When the class went back inside for circle time, he took the rock out of his pocket and was fidgeting with it. Miss Fox told him to put the rock in his cubby. Anthony shook his head *no* and began to well up with tears. She told him if he did not put it in the cubby, she would take it from him and throw it outside. He burst into tears.

I whispered in his ear to put the rock back into his pocket, because he was interrupting the circle by playing with it. He put it in his pocket and the tears subsided. My assumption was that the rock was Anthony's connection to his mother, who had dropped him off at the program four hours earlier.

When circle time was over, I asked him what he was going to do with his rock. As assumed, he said he was saving it for his mother. She was going to come pick him up at "free, free firty." His mom arrived at 5:30 that afternoon and sure enough, Anthony ran over to her as she entered. Her arms were outstretched as though waiting for him to jump into her arms for a hug and kiss. Instead, as he approached, he took out the rock and raised it into her eyes and said, "I got this for you!" To his mom's surprise and apparent disappointment, there was no hug or kiss, just a rock. To Anthony, the rock meant everything that the hug and kiss would have meant to his mother. They speak love in different languages.

I explained this to his mother and one tear streamed down her right cheek. She told me he gave her a rock every afternoon. She also told me that when they got outside, she asked him to leave it on the ground. The rock he gave her today was the same rock he had been leaving on the ground every day, because to Anthony it represented his love for his mother.

The caution, when working with children who understand they are loved through gifts, is do not nurture children with materialism. We have too many adults doing so. The child gets a thirty-dollar toy truck "because I love you." Then, that same child grows up to be of driving age and wants the thirty thousand-dollar truck, and we are not prepared to buy it. This child then says, "How come you don't love me anymore?"

Dean

Dean showed a preference toward gifts. When he would arrive on Monday, he would find a handwritten card that his teacher had left in his cubby. These cards had different messages such as, "Love you no matter what happens," or "I know I can count on you to give your best." Other days, she would slip a written message into his backpack. The cards served as the gifts. Five years have passed, and to this day, Dean still carries some of those cards with him.

QUALITY TIME

The fourth language of love is quality time.[14] During quality time, the attention of the adult and child is focused on each other and what they are doing together. There can be no interruptions. A child who seeks quality time may enjoy reading together or playing a game. She may say, "Come here; I have to show you something," or she may pull at you for attention. She may say, "You never have any time to play with me," or you may notice that she often asks for you to do something with her.

Mikayla

Mikayla is playing with her dolls upstairs in her room. All of a sudden, her mother is startled by her shrieks, "Hurry Mom, hurry! Get up here now! Hurry!"

As the terrified mother runs up the thirteen oak stairs, she pictures her child dangling out the window, holding on by her fingertips or in some other kind of danger. As the door flies open, the out-of-breath mom manages to yell, "What's wrong?"

Mikayla smiles and says, "I forgot!"

What Mikayla has done is brought her mother's attention to her in a very effective manner. She has created a quality time interaction. It is best, however, not to put children in the position of demanding quality time. Instead, it is recommended that every child have quality time built into her day.

This paragraph contains a few quick thoughts about how to create quality time. As a parent, you may choose to schedule play dates with your child. A play date is time spent together doing something that does not cost money, like taking a walk, playing ball in the backyard or talking. As a teacher or provider, you may choose to use the strategy that is called Daily News. As the children enter into the classroom or home, you ask, "Do you have any daily news that you would like to share?"

SERVICE

The last, but not least, language of love is service.[15] Children who prefer this language may ask, "Can I help you?" Toddlers who are service children cannot tie their own shoes but will help another toddler tie his. He will sit there twisting the laces around and around, never tying the shoe but feeling great in his efforts to help. The service child wants and needs to help every day.

Abby

Abby is a child who feels loved when she is asked to take the attendance card to the office. But, she is not asked to do so very often. Abby is a child many would describe as challenging. She does not complete her school work, and she makes bizarre noises while the teacher is trying to explain information to the class. Abby is the child that gets her name written on the chalkboard every day before 9:15 a.m., because she has already misbehaved. By 9:20 a.m., Abby is asked to go stand in the coatroom in the back of the class. The teacher does not realize that Abby likes the coatroom. Abby is a child that needs to move, and she can do that once she is in the coatroom. In addition, Abby likes to eat. She knows she is not going out for recess with her friends and have snack, because she will stay in to catch up on her work. In the children's coatroom are the children's backpacks. These backpacks have lunches in them. Abby rummages through the children's backpacks and chooses which one she will eat for lunch by 9:30 a.m. each day. She likes brownies and cupcakes and gets her fill. Then, she becomes disruptive again and is sent to the principal's office for further discipline.

Abby likes going to the principal's office, because the principal is rarely in the principal's office. Today, she has learned that the principal is away at a meeting. But Mrs. Oliver is in the principal's office, because she is his receptionist. Mrs. Oliver asks Abby, "Could you bring this lunch to Mr. Hernandez's room? John's mom brought it, because he forgot it." Abby is excited at this opportunity, because now she can have brunch and be of service.

Stories like this one would be minimal if adults understood Abby's need to be of service to others. This knowledge would allow adults to wisely create opportunities for her to be helpful. When adults give Abby chances to serve, they will notice that her behavior becomes less challenging.

The research of Daniel Goldman and others tells us that warm, emotional interactions help the central nervous system grow. We also know that children cannot live without a secure, positive attachment to at least one significant adult in their life. The developmental milestones cannot be reached without this "charismatic adult" or partner in the dance of interaction. When children do not have the experiences needed to master the developmental milestones that underlie their emotional well - being, they may become overwhelmed and their behaviors become difficult to channel. Therefore, we cannot leave the nurturance of children to chance. We must give our undivided attention to the languages of love and know our children well enough to honor their language.

When I first learned this information, it made so much sense. I had just finished reading the book *Silver Boxes* by Florence Littauer. In the first chapter, Mrs. Littauer is explaining to her readers that she was charged with giving a children's sermon at an old New England style church. She decided her topic would be communication. In delivering this sermon, Mrs. Littauer explained to the congregation, "that when our words come out of our mouths, they should be like presents all wrapped up to be given away." And as the story continued, "One precious little girl stood up, stepped into the aisle, and said loudly to the whole congregation, as if serving as my interpreter, "What she means is that our words should be like little silver boxes with bows on top." [16]

Having been impressed with this story, I broadened the picture from words to my own behaviors and applied what I would need to do in order to honor the languages of love in my family. I asked myself, "If I could change one thing about my behavior that would lead to a stronger emotional connection with my husband and each of my children, what would I do?" On an index card, I wrote down four ways to adjust my actions – one for each person in my family. I then folded the index card and placed it inside a quarter - pound candy box. I wrapped the box in silver wrapping paper and placed a small silver bow on top. My idea was not to give the box to these individuals but to put the box in a place where I could see it when I was in their company. The box served as a visual reminder of what I committed to change about myself.

Naively, I thought my behaviors would change quickly. Seven years later, the boxes were still within sight and to this day, I am still working on these changes. It is not important how long it takes, but that we are working diligently and moving forward. Someday, these commitments will be met.

CHAPTER 5

BEING YOUNIQUE

"A Water Bearer in China had two large pots, each hung on one of the ends of a pole that he carried across his neck. One of the pots had a crack in it, while the other pot was perfect and always delivered a full portion of water. At the end of the long walk from the stream to the house, the cracked pot arrived only half full. For two years this went on daily, with the bearer delivering only one and one - half pots of water to his house.

Of course, the perfect pot was proud of its accomplishments; perfect for which it was made. But the poor cracked pot was ashamed of its imperfection, and miserable that it was able to accomplish only half of what it was designed to do.

After two years of what it perceived to be a bitter failure, it spoke to the Water Bearer one day by the stream. 'I'm ashamed of myself because this crack in my side allows water to leak out on the way back to your house.'

The Bearer said, 'Did you notice that there are flowers only on your side of the path, and not the other? That's because I have always known about your flaw, and I planted flower seeds on your side of the path. Every day while we walked back, you watered them. For two years I have been able to pick those beautiful flowers to decorate my table. Without you being just the way you are, there would not be this beauty.' "

Chinese Fable

5

Many theories of behavior have been proposed and studied throughout the past seventy years. The temperament theory, dating back to 400 BC and the Greek philosophers, has been the longest lasting of all the theories devised. It is based on a model of four types of behavior, and has served as one of the most helpful explanations concerning what makes people tick.

For years, we have falsely believed that all children could be raised and taught using one road map. It appeared easier to guide all children as though they were the same. However, research has confirmed that children are different from birth. Each child dances to the beat of his own music. He acts, responds and reacts differently according to his biological makeup and the environments that surround him. Each child is prepackaged with the traits that, in part, determine how he will interact with his world. Since temperament is not chosen, all that is left is for us to identify, understand, accept and work with the one we have been given.

Let's look at my three children named Erin, Brett and Corey.

Erin

Erin is full of fun. She is playful and promotes enthusiasm, optimism and high energy wherever she goes. She is spontaneous, but some refer to her spontaneity as being impulsive. Erin openly expresses affection and her emotions. Her friends refer to her as "Cheer Bear." She seeks affection, approval and acceptance. Being sociable and talkative, Erin loves a party. She is a people person through and through. Her hobbies are cheerleading and shopping. When out shopping for clothes, she says, "Let's buy this one…it's fun!"

Brett

Brett is goal-oriented and driven to achieve. He is powerful and certain of his future success. "When I graduate from college, I'm going to earn lots of money." His competitive spirit has served him well in the academic and athletic arenas. He once had a sweatshirt with a logo that said, "If winning isn't important, then why do we keep score?" To Brett, winning isn't everything; it's the only thing. Brett seeks to be in control of every situation. He will not shy away from challenges. Instead, he relies on his own capabilities and resources to approach challenges with great tenacity.

Rarely will you notice a display of emotion from Brett. Many have commented, "You don't know if he had fun. He doesn't say much!"

Corey

Corey's casual and reserved attitude makes him easy to get along with. He is content, diplomatic and peaceful. Corey shows high regard and sensitivity for the needs and feelings of others. He has an innate wit and laughs abound when he uses his dry humor. Corey enjoys being around a few people at a time. The friendships he made in preschool are his two closest friends, thirteen years later. Loyalty is one of his greatest strengths. He is a great team player. Corey spends his free time playing his guitar, photographing people and places of interest to him, or exploring the outdoors.

These three children are from the same gene pool. They are brothers and sister. They live in the same home, with the same parents and have attended the same schools. Each is a tapestry of gifts with richness to contribute to others. Yet each approaches life differently.

According to Karr-Morse and Wiley, temperament is defined as a subset of personality. They say, "It is the child's basic orientation to emotions and arousal. These orientations are woven into the genetic endowment, underlie personality and shape how the child responds to learning experiences."[17] Therefore, temperament is not something that changes over time, because genetics do not change. Nevertheless, it can be refined and managed. Temperament is thought of as the single most powerful influence on behavior. It is the first influence that affects us, and it travels with us through life. Temperament directs our behavioral pattern or style. We are best advised to spend time discovering this natural style, so we can direct it, or it will direct us.

To understand this gift, we will look at the DISC Model of Human Behavior. Through this model, "We begin to understand the behavior of individuals that once baffled us. What was once bewilderment can often be replaced with amusement," according to Dr. Robert Rohm and his associates at Personality Insights, Inc. [18]

The DISC Model of Human Behavior is not meant to give a complete profile of a child's personality or to lock a child into categories or labels. It is not to be used to prejudge and use a child's weaker traits as a weapon to condemn. Nor does it provide us with an excuse to indulge in our weaknesses. The model describes behavioral tendencies and gives us a language to DISCover patterns of behavior.

If I were holding a bottle and smashed it to the floor, it would shatter into many pieces. The property of one of these pieces might be described as sharp. This sharpness could puncture, lacerate or in some way cause harm to my body or others. However, if I were to toss that glass into the ocean and find it ten, twelve or eighteen years later, would it have this same property? The answer is probably not, because the effects of the environment would have rounded off the edges to produce a smoother version of the glass. I have not swapped it for another piece of glass, just provided an environment that allowed it to become a better version of itself. Becoming a better version is a sign of maturity. This is what understanding and applying the DISC model allows us to do. We can meet children where they are and smooth them into their best. We want to work with and direct their style, instead of trying to make them into something they were never intended to become.

As we begin to unfold the model in a simplified way, we look at the pace of the individual. Some people are *active* and *outgoing*. Their internal motor is in drive, and their direction of travel is straight ahead, as quickly as possible. They have a predisposition to act like the Energizer bunny. They go and go and go and go and just keep going. They tend to draw their energy from the external world. Their primary activities appear to be achieving or having fun.

In contrast, other people are *passive* and *reserved*. Their internal motor runs at a slower pace, and at times they are "chillin'." My college roommate's father used to tell her, "You have two speeds - slow and reverse. Which one are you in now?" These individuals tend to draw their energy from their internal world. Their primary activities appear to be thinking or helping others.

The model unfolds further when we look at priority. This refers to what people chose to focus most of their attention and energies toward as they move through life. Some people are *task-oriented* individuals. They enjoy having projects to do. If you have ever been given a "honey do" list, it was probably written by a task-oriented person. These people appear to be more independent and guarded in their relationships. Alternately, others are *people-oriented* individuals. These people enjoy interacting with others.

As we begin to understand others, or ourselves, we must ask some questions. Even though you are a blend of these traits, if you had to choose between being active and outgoing or passive and reserved, what would you choose? If you had to choose between task-oriented or people-oriented, which would you choose? You may change your mind later, but for now, write down your two answers to these questions. As you continue to read, you will use your answers to gain information about your personality style.

As we view each person's *pace* and *priority*, the DISC model develops into four temperament types. An individual may be active/outgoing and task-oriented. If these two descriptors are present, this is called the "D" type. If a person's two main descriptors are active/outgoing and people-oriented,

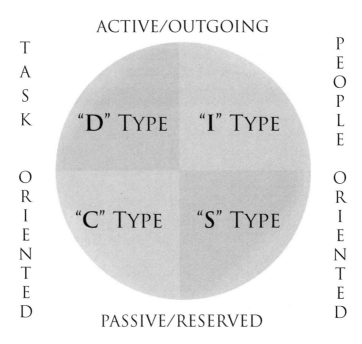

ACTIVE/OUTGOING

T
A
S
K

O
R
I
E
N
T
E
D

"D" TYPE   "I" TYPE

"C" TYPE   "S" TYPE

P
E
O
P
L
E

O
R
I
E
N
T
E
D

PASSIVE/RESERVED

this person is referred to as the "I" type. Those who are passive/reserved and people-oriented are called the "S" type. The "C" type individual is passive/reserved and task-oriented. The diagram above illustrates the model.

Looking back at the three children we mentioned earlier, Erin is an "I", Brett is a "D" and Corey is an "S". However, in reality, no one is 100% of any one type. It is more accurate to say that every person is a blend of the four types. In this blend, some traits have greater influence than others. Erin is an "I/S" blend. This means she is always people oriented, but can be active/outgoing or passive/reserved. Most often, she is active and outgoing, because the "I" is dominant. Brett is a "D/C" blend. He is always task-oriented, but can be active/outgoing or passive/reserved. Most often, he is active and outgoing. Corey is an "S/C" blend. He is always passive/reserved, but can be task-oriented or people-oriented. Predominantly, he is people-oriented.

As we study temperament, it is important to understand that one type or blend is not better than another. They are just different. Each temperament can make contributions to life, because all four have strengths. In addition, we can all grow beyond the constraint of our dominant style and learn from others how to grow in the part of our temperament that is not strong.

One of the activities I have done with parents and educators is called the BUG and BRAG List. They each draw a Franklin T on a piece of paper. On the top left of the T, they write the word BUG. Then under that word, they write down all the things that "bug" them about a child who is special to them. When the list is complete, they are instructed to move over to the next column and on the top right, write the word BRAG. Under this word, they are to write all the things about this child they can brag about to others.

BUG   BRAG

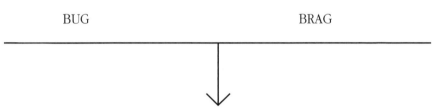

In doing this activity, the hope is that the brag list will have more things listed than the bug list. The brag list represents the child's strengths or traits when they are in control, while the bug list represents areas for improvement or traits when they are out of control. When we focus on the bug list, the child grows up to believe there is something wrong with her. There is a principle in behavior that says, "You can focus on the negative all you want, but it will never produce a positive." And so it is with children. Our goal is to learn to emphasize the natural strengths and subdue the weaknesses. Only when we focus on the positive can positive blossom.

Over the years, the strengths of many children have been highlighted through an activity called "Sweet Dreams." Using the list of one-liners to affirm children's strengths, found in the book, *Different Children, Different Needs*, written by Charles Boyd[19] (or statements of praise we have made up ourselves) we write appropriate positive statements onto a pillowcase, using a fabric marker. The child's parent is asked to read at least one of these statements to their child just before going to sleep. Research tells us that the subconscious mind never sleeps. The messages we hear just before sleep play throughout the night in the subconscious mind.

This activity has two purposes. The first is to teach children who they are. The second is to enhance the self-esteem of children, because the key to healthy self-esteem, is being accepted for who you are.

Let's revisit my three children one more time. Some people have complained about Erin's activity level and the complaint sounded like this, "What's the matter with her? Can't she sit still?" Her pillowcase would reframe that trait to sound like, "You are active, and active people get things done." This reframing moves the trait from the bug list to the brag list.

Some people questioned Brett's persistence, and the question sounded like this, "If you're such an expert in child psychology, then what's the matter with him? All he needs is one good swat to break his spirit." His pillowcase would reframe that trait to sound like, "You will be a great leader some day. You have the ability to stick with things until they are done."

Some people expressed their disappointment with Corey's passivity, and it sounded like this, "Just get him to do something... anything. Why is he so lazy?" His pillowcase would reframe that trait to sound like, "You like to do things at the same time and in the same way, because this helps you to feel peaceful."

Stephanie

Stephanie was a four-year-old child. She lived in a chaotic environment with her mother, father and three siblings. The older two siblings were teenagers and fathered by her mother's first husband. In that family, there was a history of abuse. As a result, the older children were repeating the pattern of the past and abusing the younger two children. When I met with this mom, she was ready to give the younger two children up for voluntary adoption. She was feeling less than adequate in her ability to parent and keep her children safe.

A team of fifteen professionals worked with this family for one year. One of the activities we did was "Sweet Dreams." It would be naive to think that this activity could address the complexity of the issues of this family. However, it was one of many strategies that held hope for improvement.

Pillowcases were created for each of the children and their mom read one statement each night to each of her children.

At the end of the year, it was not clear that this family would remain together. Nine years later, this mom came to a training that I offered. She walked up to me and said, "You probably don't remember me, and I'm only here to tell you one thing." I told her I did remember her and asked how all the children were doing. She started to cry, because I remembered all their names. To make a long story short, she said, "Of all the people that worked with my family, you were the only one who came every time we had an appointment. You probably told me a lot of things that could have helped, but the only thing I remember is the pillowcases you made. You believed so strongly in the things that you wrote about my kids that I thought, as their mother, that I should be able to see and believe at least one of them. The more I read them, the more I could see them. That pillowcase idea was so helpful that we have made a new pillowcase each year for the last nine years. This year, we sewed them all together, and they are the quilts on their beds."

There are many uses of the DISC model. Two of the most important are self-improvement and improving our relationships with others.

CHAPTER 6

MEETING YOUR TYPE

"Celebrate the child you have. Don't be regretful that you didn't get a different one."

Mariaemma Willis and Victoria Kindle Hudson [20]

6

"What will you teach when you graduate from here?" One of my college professors asked this question, and it shaped my future. It seemed like an easy enough question to answer since we were all studying education.

When the question was asked, one student shouted, "Physical education," while others chimed in with, "Elementary education," or "High school."

My professor emphatically replied, *"Stop! You will teach children."* The point was made. Effective education balances standards, relationships, assessment and curriculum, with individualized instruction. We must never lose sight of the child. If this is true, then why has the educational agenda of this country become overly concerned with standards, assessment and curriculum, at the expense of relationships and individualized instruction? Does this need to be a dichotomy or can we reach the balance?

Knowing and understanding each child is the heart and soul of our adult-child relationships. It is the foundation for what is called individualization or goodness of fit. This process requires us to acknowledge and accommodate to the unique abilities, interests and needs of each child. But with twenty-five to thirty children in your classroom, how can this be done?

As we journey further, we must embrace the DISC concept and investigate personality types more fully. The following information is taken from Dr. Robert Rohm. The material comes from his book,

Positive Personality Profiles and from his seminar presentations.[21] "The letter "D" (*outgoing and task-oriented*) stands for **Dominant, Driving, Demanding, Determined, Decisive** and **Doer.** The key concept to grasp is 1) Outgoing 2) Task-Oriented 3) Dominant (or other "D" type descriptive words)." "D" types have a "make it happen now" attitude! Daniel is a "D" type. At the age of three years old, he hit his chest with his hand and stated, "Me the boss!" When I asked him who was the boss in his house, he hit himself with greater emphasis, raised his voice and said, "ME THE BOSS!" And I believed him.

The letter "I" (*outgoing and people-oriented*) stands for **Inspirational, Influencing, Inducing, Impressive, Interactive, Interesting** and **Interested in people.** The key concept to grasp is 1) Outgoing 2) People - Oriented 3) Inspirational (or other "I" type descriptive words.) "I" types have a "make it fun" attitude. Sarah is an "I" type. She enters her classroom, walks up to her peers and says, "I got a new shirt. Do you like my new shirt? It's pink and orange. And look at my new sneakers. They light up; watch." She then hits the heel of her shoes on the floor to activate the lights. Everything about Sarah says, "Hey, look at me. Aren't I just the cutest thing you have ever seen?"

The letter "S" (*reserved and people-oriented*) stands for **Supportive, Submissive, Stable, Steady, Sentimental, Shy** and **Status quo.** The key concept to grasp is 1) Reserved 2) People-Oriented 3) Supportive (or other "S" descriptive words.) "S" types have an "I'll go along with you" attitude. Sam is an "S" type. His mom and dad drove over to his friend's house, where he was playing, to let him know they were going to play tennis. Sam likes to play tennis, too. When asked if he wanted to play, he said, "Well, I'm playing with Matt right now, but if it's going to hurt your feelings, I'll play tennis with you." How sweet is that?

The letter "C" (*reserved and task-oriented*) stands for **Cautious, Competent, Calculating, Concerned, Careful** and **Contemplative.** The key concept to grasp is 1) Reserved 2) Task-Oriented 3) Cautious (or other "C" type descriptive words). "C" types have a "does this make sense?" attitude. Ben is a "C" type. While lying on the beach one day, he looked at his mother and asked, "Mom, if clouds are made up of water and water is heavier than air, then why do clouds float?"

Not having an answer, she responded, "That's a great question. I don't know the answer, but they're doing a good job, so let's leave it at that."

How do we come to know our children? The long and the short of it is through observation. The skills of observation are defined as watching and listening to learn. Through observation we discern who the child is and what the child can do. Observing helps us see the world through the eyes of the child. It provides us with the information we need to build the relationships that we agree are critical to their development. Observation empowers us to plan environments that honor children, while supporting their success. And observation reveals information that we can use to determine what to teach and how to teach it.

By observing children's play and behavior, we uncover their:

- **Culture.** What language does this child speak? What types of food does he prefer? How does he dress? How does he communicate? Who are his heroes and why?

- **Temperament.** Is he active or passive? Outgoing or reserved? Task-Oriented or People-Oriented? Dominant, Inspiring, Supportive or Cautious?

- **Interests.** What does he do in his spare time? When was the last time he showed excitement toward a subject? What was the subject or topic? What does he talk, read or write about when given his choice?

- **Skills and Talents.** What does this child do well? Linguistics, Math, Art, Music, Nature or something else?

- **Approaches to Learning.** What is this child's preferred way of taking in and processing new information? Auditory? Tactile-Kinesthetic? Visual? Whole Body? Hands On? Sketching? Writing? Print? Pictures? Listening? Talking?

- **Nurturance Style.** Is this child primarily physical touch, affirmation, gifts, quality time or service?

So let's test your powers of observation. I found this activity when I was visiting the state of Maine. It is called TEST YOUR IQ. You are to read the sentence inside the box.

> FINISHED FILES ARE THE RE-
> SULT OF YEARS OF SCIENTIF-
> IC STUDY COMBINED WITH
> THE EXPERIENCE OF YEARS.

Now count the F's in the above box. Count them only once. Do not go back and count them again. How many did you count? Three, four, five or more?

There are six F's in this sentence. So how did you do with this observation? According to the scoring that accompanied this activity, three means you are so-so, four is average, five is above average and six is genius. Of course, this is just for fun. There is no connection between this activity and your intelligence. But it does highlight that we can be looking at something and not see it as it is.

Let's do one more activity.

This is called DISTINGUISHABLE CHARACTERISTICS OF A PENNY. From memory, write down all the distinguishable features you can recall having looked at and held thousands of pennies in your lifetime. Give yourself about ten minutes to complete this activity.

Now, take out a penny and compare your observations from memory to what you really see when you focus your attention. How did you do on this one?

Here are the features. On the front of a penny are IN GOD WE TRUST, LIBERTY, the date, a mintmark under the date and President Lincoln's portrait facing toward the date. On the back of the penny are UNITED STATES OF AMERICA, ONE CENT, E PLURIBUS UNUM and the Lincoln Memorial with twelve-columns and Lincoln in the columns. The general features are that it is made of copper, the diameter is three quarters of an inch, the thickness is one sixteenth of an inch, the weight is one sixth of an ounce, the front and back are inverted from each other, and there is a raised rim around the edge on both sides.

Just as many of us missed some of the details in the previous two activities, we also miss critical details about the children we work with and love. Every day, we make assumptions and judgments, recommendations and demands on children based on what we think we know about them. As Clayton Barbeau states, "Learning to pay attention is a fantastic gift. That's what's wrong with the world; there aren't enough people who pay attention to other people."[22]

There is one more technique that I have used over the years to gather information about the individuality of children. This is called a BIOPOEM. To do this activity, you will need a sheet of paper and a pen. The format for a biopoem is as follows:

(write your first name)
daughter or son of

(write the names of your parents)
who loves

(write up to 3 people, places or things you love)
who fears

(write up to 3 things that you fear)
who would like to

(write up to 3 things you would like to do, be, have or experience in the next one to five years)
who lives in

(write the name of your city and state)

(write your last name)

OVERVIEW OF THE DISC MODEL [23]

D TYPES ARE:	I TYPES ARE:	S TYPES ARE:	C TYPES ARE:
Dominant	Inspiring	Supportive	Cautious
Demanding	Influencing	Steady	Competent
Decisive	Inducing	Stable	Cognitive
Doer	Impressive	Secure	Calculating
Determined	Impressionable	Sweet	Critical Thinker
Direct	Interested	Submissive	Consistent
Diligent	Imaginative	Shy	Conscientious
Director	Impulsive	Sentimental	Correct
And may be:	*And may be:*	*And may be:*	*And may be:*
Defiant	Illogical	A Sucker	Cold

D TYPES WANT:	I TYPES WANT:	S TYPES WANT:	C TYPES WANT:
Results	Affection	Peace	Information
	Fun	Stability	Quality
	Excitement		

D TYPES NEED:	I TYPES NEED:	S TYPES NEED:	C TYPES NEED:
Control	Attention	Security	Quality answers
Challenges	Approval	Appreciation	Procedures
		Support	Time for analysis and thinking

D TYPES DO NOT LIKE:	I TYPES DO NOT LIKE:	S TYPES DO NOT LIKE:	C TYPES DO NOT LIKE:
Indecision	Schedules	Insensitivity	Being criticized
Slow pace	Being ignored	Conflict	Mistakes
Waiting	Repetitive tasks	Sarcasm	Sudden changes
Laziness	Details	Surprises	Interruptions
Details	Long-term	Unclear	Disorganization
Taking orders	projects	expectations	Superficiality
All talk, no action	Being isolated or excluded	Tension-filled environments	Illogical decisions
Displays of emotion		Rushing	Injustice

D TYPES LIKE:	I TYPES LIKE:	S TYPES LIKE:	C TYPES LIKE:
To win To plan New ideas To be in charge To move To be challenged Physical activities Achieving	To be liked To express themselves Being in a group Surprises Social activities Recognition Playing Being creative	Belonging Teamwork Cooperation Predictability Harmony Things that are familiar Calmness Watching	To be right To know the expectations Established routines Clear directions Finishing Planning Organizing Things done right Rules obeyed
D TYPES WANT YOU TO BE:	**I TYPES WANT YOU TO BE:**	**S TYPES WANT YOU TO BE:**	**C TYPES WANT YOU TO BE:**
Quick To the point A winner	Fun Upbeat Enthusiastic Responsive Stimulating	Kind Pleasant Patient Understanding Sensitive	Accurate Accountable Analytical Serious Literal Organized
D TYPES SPARK CONFLICT BY:	**I TYPES SPARK CONFLICT BY:**	**S TYPES SPARK CONFLICT BY:**	**C TYPES SPARK CONFLICT BY:**
Being intolerant or insensitive Using tactless, blunt communication Becoming overly competitive or aggressive Being too independent or detached Moving too quickly	Clowning around Talking too much Interrupting Being Pollyanna Lacking attention to detail Being disorganized Being overly excitable or emotional Being manipulative	Resisting change Being indecisive Maintaining a slow pace Lacking initiative Resisting new ideas Being nonassertive	Being critical or judgmental Worrying Acting suspicious Being intolerant of mistakes Hiding emotions Not socializing Becoming overly analytical

D TYPES OUT OF CONTROL APPEAR:	**I** TYPES OUT OF CONTROL APPEAR:	**S** TYPES OUT OF CONTROL APPEAR:	**C** TYPES OUT OF CONTROL APPEAR:
Reckless	Unrealistic	Dependent	Compulsive
Rude	Manipulative	Clingy	Critical
Impatient	Emotional	Indecisive	Unsociable
Pushy	Gossipy	Uncommunica-	Fearful
Dictatorial/Bossy	Impulsive	tive	Worrisome
Conceited	Unfocused	Inflexible	Rigid
Arrogant	Distractible	Easily	Doubtful
Offensive	Purposeless	manipulated	Nit Picky
Abrasive		Lacking initiative	
		Resistant	
D TYPES UNDER CONTROL APPEAR:	**I** TYPES UNDER CONTROL APPEAR:	**S** TYPES UNDER CONTROL APPEAR:	**C** TYPES UNDER CONTROL APPEAR:
Courageous	Optimistic	Relaxed	Organized
Results-Oriented	Persuasive	Reliable	Logical
Deliberate	Excites	Cooperative	Intense
Self-Confident	Communicative	Steadfast	Curious
Self-reliant	Spontaneous	Softhearted	Cautious
Straightforward	Outgoing	Systematic	Questioning
Assertive	Involved	Amiable	Precise
	Friendly	Good listener	Conscientious

CHAPTER 7

HAVING A FIT

"The majority of kids go to bed every night wishing they had been heard."

Mariaemma Willis and Victoria Kindle Hudson [24]

7

The Dance of Interaction is not a solo performance with the adult as the director. The patterns of interaction between the adult and child take the spotlight in the production.

In gardening, we understand that different plants need different nutrients. When we provide those nutrients, we reap the results of our effort. We understand that providing what is needed to each one will eventually add beauty to the world. We can sit back and enjoy the color, the fragrance and the gentleness of the flowers blowing in the wind. Yet, so often when it comes to relationships, we practice a form of egocentricity. We do not think that different children with their unique styles will need different environments and approaches. Consciously or unconsciously, we create a biased environment and adhere to a rigidity and intolerance that is based on our own style. Thus, we behave in ways that meet our own needs.

Research has confirmed that "D" type individuals comprise 10% of the population of the world, "I" types represent 30%, "S" types represent 35% and "C" types represent 25%. (These are approximate figures.) Knowledge of the percentages helps parents and teachers to evaluate their natural tendencies to (potentially) effectively interact with each segment of the population. For example, I am a "C/D/S" blend. (That means that I have more "C" tendencies and traits than any other of the three styles. Next comes "D" and then "S". By leaving the "I" off the description of my blend, I am saying that I have very few "I" traits in my personality. (The styles I list when I describe my personality style also explain which styles are above the midline on my personality assessment. Therefore, the "I" style is below the midline on the assessment.[25] Being a "C/D/S" blend, I naturally have some ability to relate to 70% of the population. ("C" types are 25%, "D" types are 10% and "S" types are 35%. Add those figures, and the result is 70%.) If I did not have this awareness or if I consciously chose not to change my behavior or the environment, I would have created a bias against 30% of the population.

Relating this to my role as a teacher, what would I say to the 30% of the children that I am naturally biased against? "Wait until next year to be nurtured?"

Relating this to my role as a mother, what would I say to my high "I" daughter, Erin?

Relating this to my role as a wife, what would I say to my high "I" husband, Todd?

What would *your* bias factor be? Here are two more examples to help clarify the process. When you are a "D/C" blend (your "C" and your "D" are both above the midline on a personality assessment), your bias factor is 65%. ("D" is 10%, and "C" is 25%. You relate rather well to 35% of the population. Take 35% and subtract from 100 to get 65%. There is a great likelihood that you will not relate to 65% of the population, without adjustments.) When you are a "D/I" blend, your bias factor is 60%. Looking at these examples, how can you afford this in your roles and relationships?

The Temperament Program was started in LaGrande, Oregon. This program developed an approach to parenting based on temperament traits. The program found that adjustments based on the temperament model had three outcomes.[26] The first was that conflicts and tensions in relationships were reduced. (Conflict is often a by-product of a lack of understanding and a lack of sensitivity toward others. It results from two people with opposing weaknesses attempting to interact. People frequently have trouble accepting another person's weakness when it falls within their area of strength. Acceptance takes some effort.) The second and third outcomes of the Temperament Program were that the adults enjoyed their time with children more, and there were stronger ties in the relationships.

Temperament information (personality style information) provides us with insights into what makes others tick: how they perceive the world, how they gather knowledge and learn, how they communicate, how they make decisions and how they relate to others. This knowledge then allows us to love all people equally, but treat each one differently. We can step out of our own story and experience the other person's biography.

Visiting a Preschool Classroom

Let's look at how this lack of adjustment unfolds as children interact in a preschool classroom during the transition from play to cleaning up and then to going outside to play. I have been asked to come and observe a classroom with twenty children and two teachers. One teacher is a high "S", while the other is high "C". The first child arrives by 7:30 a.m., and the last child leaves at 5:30 p.m. The time of day we will be describing is between 10:30 and 11:00 a.m.

As the observation begins, there are four children playing in the dramatic play area. This is an area that seems to be enjoyed by predominantly "I" type children. All of the children are wearing dress-up clothing. Jason has on a cowboy vest and cowboy boots. Paula is wearing a pink bathrobe and slippers. She is carrying a small red purse. Jacqueline is wearing a leather jacket, while Joseph has a firefighter smock on with his head coming out the opening meant for his arm. Joseph tells Paula to make him breakfast. He wants eggs and spaghetti with his coffee. Jason has just finished vacuuming the floor; he now takes the baby stroller and pushes it around the entire classroom at a quick pace. Round and round he goes for the next 25 minutes. There is no baby in the stroller, and Jason does not seem to be aware that he is bumping into furniture and people while running over toys. Five times the high "C" teacher says, "Jason, slow down. Go slow, Jason. Jason, show me slow." (My first thought was Jason does not know "slow." It is not part of his pace.) Jacqueline gets hit by the stroller and begins chasing Jason. Both children are laughing and running throughout the room. Now, the high "C" teacher is saying, "STOP! That's not safe. You need to slow down!" The two children appear not to hear her and continue running.

There are six children playing in the block-building area. This is an area enjoyed by predominantly "D" type children. Christopher is playing alone. He piles blocks onto a truck and drives around the classroom. Emily and Allison are playing together. They are building a castle. Along comes

Christopher to dump his load of blocks and reload. Crash! He dumps the blocks right on top of the castle. Emily pushes Christopher and round one begins. Allison yells, "They're fighting!" The teacher runs to break up the fight. Meanwhile, three others are building a tower. While the fighting is happening, their tower crashes. It appears as though there are six "D" type children who are now experiencing varying degrees of anger or disappointment.

The high "S" teacher resorts to redirection. Each child is sent to another area of the room to cool off. Christopher is sent to the book area. Immediately, the books become action novels. Christopher is tossing them around the room like Frisbees. Emily is sent to the listening center. She refuses to go there and instead, she walks to her cubby and sits in it while covering her body with her coat. Allison is sent to the easel to paint. She picks up the brush and dips it into the paint container then splatters paint on a child sitting at the table near the easel. (By now I'm sure you have the picture. The classroom is in chaos.)

There are five children playing with puzzles at the table that is near the easel. These are predominantly "C" type and "S" type children. There are minor squabbles over sharing, but for the most part, things are progressing smoothly until Jack is hit with the paint from Allison's brush. He dissolves into tears and says, "My mom is going to kill me. I'm not supposed to get my clothes dirty." With the impending potential for conflict to erupt, three children wander away from this area and find a quieter place in the room.

The remainder of the children in the room are "S" type children. They are distributed in the following way: There is one child in a private, cozy, soft place reading a book. One child is sitting on the floor sucking her fingers. The three remaining children are playing a memory match game.

Once all the conflicts are resolved, the high "C" teacher walks over to the light switch and flicks the lights off and on. This is the warning that in five more minutes, it will be time to clean up and get ready to go outside. However, to the "D" and "I" children, it means it is time to clean up now. The "D" children run to their cubbies and get their coats. The teacher says, "You need to come back over here and clean up these toys." One high "D" child, named Kevin, crosses his arms over his chest and responds, "I didn't play there."

Christopher, another high "D" child, runs around the classroom telling the other children to clean up. When they do not respond to his orders, he tells the teacher, "They're not cleaning up." He has not put one thing away himself. Instead, he has positioned himself as the self - appointed supervisor.

Another high "D" child named Rena announces, "Those aren't my toys."

The high "C" teacher firmly states, "I saw you playing there, and unless you clean these up, you will not be going outside." And, the power struggle begins.

The "I" children begin to throw all the toys into the refrigerator, stove, hutch or any other place that the toys cannot be seen. Then, they run around the classroom telling all the other children to hurry up. They do not realize the light signal was just the five-minute warning. (Those who work with preschool-age children know that once the clean-up process is complete, you can look into the refrigerator in the dramatic play area and see naked babies next to the play food and dishes. It takes too long for the "I" children to dress those babies and put them to sleep in the cradle. And it takes too long to put the food neatly away in the refrigerator or cabinet, so it ends up in the sink or cradle, as well.)

The "C" and "S" children are slower paced and reserved. They are appreciating the fact that they have a five-minute warning. They begin to plan how they are going to clean up their mess and all the other messy areas of the room.

The lights flicker off and on again. This time it really is clean-up time. All the high "I" and "D" children run to be the first ones in line. The high "C" teacher tells them, "Use your walking feet." They ignore her as they push and shove and attempt to cut in line. Each one jockeys for a favored position, with each high "D" attempting to give orders and be the line leader.

The assigned line leader is one of the slower-paced "C" children who is busy putting all the blocks away perfectly. To Jalene, all the shapes and sizes must match and this precision takes time. She ignores the children in line with their coats on as they loudly call to their peers, "Come on; hurry up! We're sweating."

The teacher is patiently telling the children in line, "We can't leave yet. We're waiting for all of our friends."

Amanda says, "They're not my friends."

The high "S" teacher replies, "We're all friends here." And on, and on the story goes…. Twenty minutes have passed, and all the children are ready to walk down the hall to go outside.

The previous scenario describes thirty minutes of a ten-hour day. Chaos abounds when we do not understand personality styles, anticipate problems and plan for success. Understanding and applying the insights gained through DISC would have led to more positive outcomes for the children and their teachers.

We have learned that "D" and "I" children love to move. When the only indoor opportunity is found in dramatic play (pushing strollers or vacuum cleaners) and blocks (driving trucks, building castles and towers), the "D" and "I" children will crowd into these areas. (This crowding can lead to the chaos described in the previous scenario.) Therefore, it may be necessary to create more than one dramatic play or block-building area, so the children spread out around the room. This may serve to decrease crowding and the conflicts and behaviors that can follow. In addition, it may be possible to increase the gross motor learning opportunities in the classroom by teaching concepts through movement exploration.

The transition may have gone more smoothly if the teachers acknowledged the differences of pace in the children. It is possible to stagger the transition, so the slower-paced children are given more than a five-minute warning to plan their clean - up activities. They can begin cleaning, before the quick-paced children are told about the transition. This allows all the children to be ready at approximately the same time, so waiting is minimized or eliminated. Another option would be to have one of the teachers adjust her style to a quicker pace and take the quick-paced children outside when they are ready, and the other teacher can stay behind to work with the slower-paced children. A third option would be for each child to sit at the table after cleaning up. One of the teachers could keep the children at the table busy singing songs with simple hand movements until everyone is ready to go outside.

Avoiding Power Struggles

The power struggle between the teacher and Rena may have been minimized or eliminated if she acknowledged the "D" child's need for control. Using words like "no, stop, don't, can't and wait" may trigger a power struggle. So when she tells a "D" child she cannot go outside if she did not clean up, instead of using a problem-solving approach or the principle of anticipation, the struggle begins. She might have said, "In five minutes, we will be going outside, but right now it is time to clean up. Would you like me to help you get started, or can you do it yourself?" Or knowing that "D" children enjoy a challenge, she may have said, "I will pick up five things in the next minute. How many do you think you can do?"

If the teacher chooses to challenge the "D" child, the child will pick up more toys than his teacher does, because it is a contest to be won. And, once completed, he raises his arms over his head and shouts, "I won!"

Challenging a "D" child is what we mean when we talk about individualization. It is anticipating the predictable patterns and designing a plan in order to create greater compatibility between the needs, capacities, and styles of children and the environment, including the adult's style. When we achieve goodness of fit, it enhances the child's strengths while helping him overcome his natural vulnerabilities. The need to tailor experiences to the individual differences is particularly important in the early education years. The alternative is the bias factor discussed previously, which results in increased levels of stress and an increased likelihood of problem behaviors. Therefore, as informed educators, we are called upon to use the DISC model and our insights to promote healthy development in all children, not just those that fit into our style or those that more easily fit into our own patterns. We must develop the art of adaptability.

Jack

Let's look at an example from the home environment. Jack is a high "S" child. His mother is a high "D" parent. This means that there will be natural conflicts involving pace and priority. One of those conflicts occurs at their home every morning.

The day begins at 7:00 when Jack's mother wakes him. He is then to get out of bed, clean himself up, get dressed, have breakfast and get ready to leave for the school bus by 8:15. To a high "D" parent, one and a quarter hours is more than ample time to achieve all of these tasks. To a high "S" child, the time is short and the tasks are numerous. He would prefer to spend some time waking up before meeting the demands of the day.

At 7:15, Jack is still in bed. His mother yells, "COME ON. HURRY UP! LET'S GO. WE'RE GOING TO BE LATE AGAIN." (Yelling is not the best choice for communicating with any child; however, it is particularly wounding to the tender heart of an "S" child. It will interfere with an "S" doing his best, and it will also affect an "S" child's self-concept.)

Jack slowly puts his feet on the floor and sits on the edge of his bed for another five minutes, all the while stretching and rubbing his eyes. He then hears his mother calling to him, "Jack, are you up yet? Come on. Let's get a move on."

Since breakfast is ready, Jack joins his family members at the table. Within two minutes of sitting down, the others leave the table, because they are done with their meal. At 7:30, Jack begins to eat. Again, Jack hears his mom's impatient words, "COME ON, JACK! HURRY. WE'RE GOING TO BE LATE. LET'S GO!" Jack experiences feelings of insecurity as he hears his mother's volume and tone.

At 7:57, Jack has finished his breakfast. Now, it's off to the bathroom to wash up, brush his teeth and comb his hair. There are eighteen minutes left before the bus arrives. It has taken him fifty-seven minutes to get out of bed and eat his breakfast. His mother begins hearing the music "To Dream the Impossible Dream" in her head. But Jack finishes in the bathroom in record time - seven minutes. Perhaps the dream will become a reality today.

At his mother's prodding, Jack runs to his room to get dressed. Jack cannot decide what he wants to wear. His favorite pants are in the laundry. The first pair he tries on are too tight, so he tries on a second pair. He settles for the second after some pouting. Soon after Jack's mom tied his shoes, Jack reappears in front of his mother and places his right foot down in front of his left. Then he stands still looking at her. Since she tied his shoes just a moment ago, she is confused. After a few seconds, she asks, "What, Jack? What do you want?"

Slowly and methodically, Jack taps her on the arm and says, "M-O-M. M-O-M."

Losing her last ounce of patience, she shouts, "WHAT?"

He looks at her in dismay and hurt because of her loudness and directness and quietly says, "M-O-M, This one is bigger than that one," while pointing to the loops that make the bow on his shoe. (His mother had quickly tied his shoe and one side of the bow was bigger than the other. He wanted them the same size.)

His mother is exasperated by his behavior. She tries to calm herself by thinking, "Remember - unconditional love." But her plan to calm down is destroyed when new thoughts begin tumbling into her head, "But if he doesn't hurry up, I'm going to kill him." She uses every bit of patience that she can muster as she grits her teeth and prods, "Jack, Come on. Hurry up! Let's GO NOW!" Jack stares at her and falls limply to the floor as though there are no bones or muscles in his body. His mom yells, "JACK, GET UP NOW AND GET MOVING OR I WILL HELP YOU!" Jack doesn't move.

Behaviorally, Jack's behavior is described as noncompliance. This means he did not initiate an appropriate response to his mother's directions within a reasonable period of time. However, understanding temperament allows one to step back and realize there is a difference in pace and priority. The truth is that Jack is not trying to be difficult. (In fact, "S" children naturally want to be helpful.) Jack is overwhelmed with trying to adapt to the quick pace of his mother. Therefore, the differences in the natural style of the mother and son have led to "poorness of fit" and stress for both parties involved.

To eliminate this morning torment, Jack now gets up thirty minutes earlier and is given fifteen minutes to warm up to the world. His clothes and backpack are prepared the evening before, so all he has to do is clean up, get dressed, eat breakfast and leave. The stress is minimized, and his mom no longer receives phone calls from his teacher.

I mention the phone calls, because on the second day of kindergarten, his mom received a call from Mrs. Holtz, Jack's teacher. She said, "We have to talk about Jack."

Curious about what they would have to talk about, his mom asked, "About what?"

Mrs. Holtz replied, "Well, today we were doing morning meeting, and I asked the children to introduce themselves to each other. When I got to Jack and asked him his name, he said, 'COME ON. HURRY UP. LET'S GO JACK!' " (Jack had heard this so many times that it appeared he considered this his name.)

Adjusting

The heart of adjustment lies in honoring your style and that of the child. In order to do so, you must identify each, then ask yourself:

1. Do I really respect all children equally, or just a particular type?

2. Am I asking a child to adjust to my style, or am I adjusting to the child's needs?

3. To what temperament does my environment and style accommodate most easily?

4. Have I created a style-biased environment?

When your goal becomes to create a bias-free environment, you will:

• Recognize your personal values, beliefs and perceptions and sort out how these cloud, confuse or interfere with your objectivity.

• Spend more time focusing on the strengths of the child.

• Adjust your style to relate to the needs of the child.

LEARNING THE DANCE STEPS

When prevention becomes the focus, as it should be, we shift from suppressing the child to changing the environment and ourselves. In doing so, we recognize that each child's expression of temperament and individual needs call for individualized solutions. These solutions may be found in positive guidance.

Positive guidance means:

- *Believing in the potential of every child.*
- *Creating a balanced environment.*
- *Teaching life skills.*
- *Using discipline techniques that are focused on solutions and are instructive in nature.*
- *Using practices that treat children with respect.*

Positive guidance means the adults influence but do not control the child; every child must learn to control himself. This implies that we must establish an environment that sets a structure, without becoming critical, demanding and controlling. In addition, we must be supportive without becoming too lenient, acquiescing and ineffective. The structure shows respect for the needs of the adult, while the support shows respect for the needs of the child.

CHAPTER 8

THERE'S NO PLACE LIKE HOME

"Creating a warm, caring, supportive, encouraging environment is probably the most important thing you can do for children."

Stephen Covey[27]

8

P revention has a lot to do with the environment we create for children. This environment, when designed well, is part of indirect guidance, because it creates a buffer against behavioral challenges. Join me as we complete another activity to illustrate the influence of environment.

On a piece of paper, draw the Franklin T. On the top left side, write the word "pro." On the top right side, write the word "con."

PRO	CON

Now, think about the store where you shop for groceries. In the PRO column, list all the things you like about this store. Next, in the CON column, list all the things that you dislike about this store. Once completed, the lists may look something like this.

PRO	CON
Clean	Cannot find what you want
Variety	Lines at the deli
Friendly, helpful staff	Not conveniently located
Background music	Not enough staff

The question is how does what we want in an environment differ from what children seek from their environment? I would submit they do not differ. Children want an environment that is clean. They like having enough toys that afford them choices about what they want to pursue. They enjoy being in the presence of adults who are friendly and helpful. According to research, children respond to adults from whom they receive approval. And, the environment reduces stress when it includes soft, background music.

On the other hand, children do not like disorganization or having to ask the adults to find everything for them. They dislike having to wait in lines or not being able to get attention from the adults when they need it. And the list goes on. I'm sure you see the point.

There are four major components that comprise the environment. It works like an ecosystem - each component is interdependent upon the others for balance.

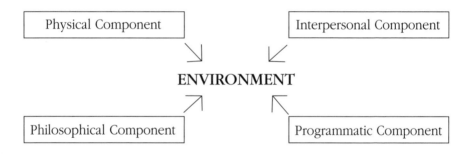

THE PHYSICAL ENVIRONMENT

This component refers to the physical space, and this space communicates messages to the children in it. According to Elizabeth Prescott and James Greenman, adults and children inhabit different worlds. As adults, "What we often don't notice are the elements that a child will zoom in on: the right place with the right shape, like a tight angular corner between the wall and the couch or the excitement of a perch; the right sight and sound, like a vantage point from which to watch and hear the torrential rain pouring out of the gutter and splashing to the ground below; or the right feel. We, who don't inhabit the floor, undervalue the hot, sunny spot on the floor that draws cats and babies. We are not drawn to the pile of dirt or the hole, to the puddle or dew, or to the rough spot where the plaster is chipping away that beckons small fingers. Our cold, utilitarian eyes assess for order and function, cleanliness and safety. We assess how the space will bend to our will…" [28] Therefore, to design effective spaces for children, we must answer the question, "Who am I creating this space for?"

Infants

In creating a balanced environment for infants, we must ask the question, "What do babies need in order to develop?" The answer is more complex than one might think. Since each infant is a unique blend of temperament traits and giftedness, no two will develop in exactly the same way and at the same pace. However, we know there are certain aspects that are universal.

• A physical environment for infants must be safe from all potential dangers, because babies learn by exploring the environment using all five senses. If they can reach it, there is a great probability it will end up in their nose, ears, mouth or eyes.

• The atmosphere must be family-like and look like a home. This supports an infant's sense of safety and security. By home-like, we refer to carpeting on the floor, pictures of their families and mirrors hung at their eye level, a rocking chair, large pillows on the floor, nonpoisonous, hanging plants and board books or picture books in every area of the room.

• Spaces that nurture mobility are a must, because infancy is the developmental stage for emerging motor skills. Smaller movement and exploration areas are more effective than large, open spaces.

Toddlers

The physical environment for toddlers (18 months to 3 years) must acknowledge the need to learn with their whole body. Toddlers are at a peak of curiosity and spend their time exploring everyone and everything. And, toddlers have an abundance of energy to expend throughout the day.

In addition, toddlers have an incredible drive for independence and doing things themselves.

Anyone who has spent time with a toddler knows that toddlers enjoy dropping things, banging, throwing, dumping and clearing off shelves, screaming, climbing and poking his fingers into small spaces or messy materials. Carol Gestwicki has written, "In designing physical environments for toddlers, it may be important first to consider several key components that must be present. There is a need for safety, as mobile, curious toddlers must be protected from their own impulsiveness and immaturity without frustrating them with unnecessary restriction. There is a need for flexibility, as the environment must keep step with children's changing needs and provide spaces that must be used for several purposes, such as play, as well as routine caregiving, new walkers, and restless climbers. There is a need for variety, to provide for different toddlers doing different things and individual exploring, as well as for expanding the world beyond the confines of the four walls. There is a need for easily restorable order, since exploration becomes an untidy process; yet toddlers need the security of familiar objects being in familiar places. There is a need for organization, so adults can help toddlers succeed at self-help, and so frustrating waits can be minimized. There is a need for challenge, as bored toddlers are more likely to get involved in undesirable behaviors."[29]

Preschoolers

Preschoolers (ages 3-5 years) approach life with an avid curiosity about the larger world and how it works. Play dominates their days. According to Isenberg and Jalongo, "Play enables children to create understandings of their world from their own experiences and exerts a strong influence on all aspects of their growth and development. Children become empowered in play to do things for themselves, to feel in control, to test and practice their skills and to affirm confidence in themselves. Play is important for children's developing sense of competence."[30]

In 1984, Elizabeth Prescott described seven dimensions that create a balanced environment for young children. When these seven are in balance, the environment supports play as the primary vehicle for learning and the healthy development of young children.

PRESCOTT'S DIMENSIONS[31]

Softness/Hardness

Softness in an environment is provided for by the presence of objects (finger paints, play dough, clay, couches, pillows, rugs, grass, water, sand, dirt, animals that can be held) that are soft, malleable, and responsive to touch, providing a variety of tactile sensory stimulation.

Hardness (tiled floors, wooden furniture, asphalt playgrounds) gives a more unyielding message, one that encourages children to shape themselves to the environment, inevitably tiring and stress - inducing for both children and adults.

A balance means the environment is both responsive and resistant.

Open/Closed

Openness in an environment is perceived by the presence of open equipment and materials; those that can be used in a variety of ways, with no one correct way of using them, and no arbitrary stopping point. Sand, blocks, collage, and other art materials are all open. Activity formats may also be open, based primarily on children choosing from a selection of activities planned and prepared by the teacher. The issue of openness is related to choices.

Closed materials can only be played with in one way; puzzles and various Montessori materials are closed. Program styles that utilize mostly teacher-directed group and individual activities are called closed, as are experiences that have a clear ending.

The balance for young children is toward openness.

Simple/Complex

The simplest play unit has only one aspect, and one obvious use; there is nothing to improvise in its use. An example would be a swing. More complex units combine two different kinds of materials; supercomplex units combine three different kinds of materials. Examples of complexity include adding shovels to sand or rolling pins to play dough; supercomplex would add water and molds to sand, or decorative elements to the play dough and rollers. A supercomplex dramatic play area adds cookbooks, pads for grocery lists, aprons, and telephone books.

Complexity in play holds the interest of children for longer periods of time.

Intrusion/Seclusion

An environment introduces the dimensions of intrusion and seclusion as it defines boundaries and provides opportunities for privacy and control over personal belongings and space. In the environment, children should use spaces that are shared by the group. It is also important that there are spaces where children can be alone, and to safeguard their personal property and interests.

Desirable intrusion comes when the child makes connections to what the larger world is about, such as having windows that connect to the outdoor space, and having visitors in the classroom.

High Mobility/ Low Mobility

This dimension of an environment concerns the freedom children have to move around. With high mobility, there is space and equipment to encourage gross motor skills, active movement, such as running, climbing, and dancing. With low mobility, children are required to sit still for activities, such as storytime or working on puzzles.

A balanced environment provides space and materials for both.

Risk/Safety

There is a need for both risk and safety in an environment. While children need to be protected from obvious dangers and taught safety practices, the environment must not overlook important opportunities for risk - taking, such as opportunities to experiment with bodies in space: climbing and jumping off.

There is a difference between providing for safety by teaching children how to do interesting and challenging things with care, rather than forbidding any kind of risk or innovation, because it is unsafe.

Large Group/ Individual

There is a need for balance in the social structure within the environment, and not an overbalance or omission of either dimension. A large group experience involves groups of five - the majority of children, but not all; an individual experience is being read to one - on - one. Small group experiences involve two to four children at a time. Full group means everyone together.

School-age children

School-age children spend their time becoming a member of their society. They are ready to take on more responsibility and be seen as competent. Therefore, the physical environment for this developmental stage must nurture those feelings of competence.

THE INTERPERSONAL ENVIRONMENT

The interpersonal environment refers to the relationships (child-child, adult-child and adult-adult). It encompasses our style of providing care to children, including communication style, conflict resolution approaches and methods of discipline we choose to use. It is about the attitude we bring to parenting or teaching and our willingness to meet the needs of our children.

Many experts have studied the continuum of providing care to children (Ainsworth, Bowlby, et al.), and their work leads us to believe there are four possible approaches on this continuum: (1) authoritarian (2) permissive by consent (3) permissive by default (4) authoritative.

Authoritarian caregivers

Authoritarian caregivers often react to children and their behaviors, rather than respond. This approach attempts to control and suppress the child because of a strong drive for things to be orderly and perfect. Conformity and blind obedience to their authority are the ultimate goals. The authoritarian adult must be in control, and being in control means making all the decisions.

The authoritarian style is high in demands and rules and low in nurturance and responsiveness to the emotions and ideas of the child. In fact, emotions may be denied or dismissed. When the child cries, the adult may say, "Stop crying. There's nothing to cry about. Only babies cry." Authoritarian individuals tend to focus on what they themselves want instead of what the child may need.

Adults using the authoritarian style tend to use hidden or destructive styles of communication. Their messages may not be clearly delivered. Some of the communication methods include:

- Blaming. "I hope you're satisfied now. We have to leave the beach because of you." Blaming creates distance in our relationship and puts the child on the defensive.

- Intellectualizing. In this method, there is little display of emotion and big words are used to avoid the real issue. "I can explain everything to you, but you need to stop interrupting me while I'm talking! I'm very wise, you know."

- Distracting. Here real issues are avoided by changing the subject to something irrelevant. A child may be upset, because she cannot complete her project. She does not have enough materials to do so. Instead of helping her get the materials, this adult says, "You don't need that right now. Let's go finish throwing the ball around and forget about it."

- Criticizing. An authoritarian adult may make negative, critical comments even when the child is doing what he is supposed to be doing. For example, "Michael, it's about time you hit the ball. We worked on it long enough." This adult considers these types of comments encouraging.

- Ordering. This style directs and runs roughshod over children. Ordering means the child is told how to feel, how to think and how to behave. "You will go to soccer practice, because you love soccer. You will have a great time while you are there, and you will thank me when you are done."

Adults in the authoritarian style tend to rely on punishment and the use of anger to control the child, instead of discipline techniques to address the child's behaviors. Using these methods represents an overuse or misuse of authority and power. This approach tends to humiliate the child. Authoritarian strategies include putting the child in the corner, writing the child's name on the board, spanking, shaking, yelling, using threats ("You better come right now, or I'll leave you here.") and using sarcasm or guilt. ("You should be ashamed of yourself. I tell you over and over. When will you ever get it? What's wrong with you?") These strategies are based on coercion and fear and are usually followed up by one of these statements, "I'm doing this for your own good," or, "This hurts me more than it hurts you." Conflicts are usually resolved in a win-lose style. The adult wins, and the child loses, because the adult is more concerned with who is right, than what is right. This style proves that the adult is bigger and stronger, but at what cost? What is the result in terms of the trust and respect in the relationship?

Authoritarian adults may use one additional strategy - withholding affection. When the child comes home later than expected, the parent gives a dirty look, shakes her head, but says nothing. There is no discussion or feedback. The silence is meant to control the child's thoughts and emotions.

According to the experts, this approach with children may produce conflicted-irritable children. The emotions they are not allowed to express are building up inside, and these may surface someday. When they do, they may show themselves as loud demands, active rebellion or passive-aggressive patterns. Some of the resulting traits are fearfulness and apprehension around authority figures, moodiness, a vulnerability to stress, a lack of self-confidence, lower social skills, and higher levels of manipulative, rebellious or aggressive behaviors.

Permissive caregivers

The permissive caregivers often ignore or give in to the child or his behaviors, rather than respond. They believe that children should be allowed to make their own decisions and control their own behavior, even when the child lacks the knowledge and maturity to do so.

There are two types of permissive styles and both have weakly established boundaries or no boundaries at all. The demands and structure are low. However, these two styles differ in their degree of responsiveness and nurturance.

Permissive by choice caregivers

The permissive by choice style is low in demands and structure but high in support and nurturance. Adults in this style believe children have rights that are never to be interfered with by adults. They avoid imposing any controls and instead, tolerate children's impulses, even aggressive ones. I saw an example of this style recently when I was shopping in a store and a mom entered, carrying her child who appeared to be about 18 months old. As she looked for inkjet refills, her son punched her three times in the face. She did nothing in response to this aggressive behavior. She never got a carriage to put him in or turned him away from her or put him down. She did not say one word. She continued to look for her cartridge.

Permissive by default caregivers

The permissive by default style is low in demands and structure, and low in responsiveness and nurturance. These individuals are permissive, because their methods of discipline have been ineffective. As a result, they have a tendency to give up, and let the child get his way. I saw an example of this when I was visiting a family at their request, because Joshua was "out of control," as they described him. It was 4:00 p.m. Joshua asked his mother if he could have a snack. His mom replied, "No, we'll be eating supper soon." Joshua pulled a chair over to the counter, climbed up and got himself a bag of potato chips from the cabinet. He then opened the refrigerator and pulled out a two-liter bottle of soda. He took the chips and soda into the living room. He sat on the couch watching television, eating the chips and drinking the soda from the bottle.

I asked his mom if that was ok with her. She asked, "Why?"

I replied, "Because I thought I heard you say *no* to the snack."

She said, "Well, what do you want me to do? If I don't let him have it now, he'll get up during the night and help himself."

I gently shared with her, "You want what is best for your child. I know that you want a lifestyle for your son that is better or equal to the one that you have. Would you be open to me sharing information with you that would help you with your parenting?"

The mother eagerly said, "Yes."

I then continued, "In parenting, we try to do what is in the best interest of the child. If you allow your son to break the rules without negative consequences, he will experience much more difficulty in life. He will get his way for the moment, but he will become an unhappy child. If, on the other hand, you are firm and do not allow your son to break the rules, it will help him to gain self-control in all areas of his life. If he becomes obedient, all of his relationships will become smoother, and he will be happier and more successful in life."

To permissive caregivers, the word "no" does not mean *no*. It means "maybe," just keep asking. As a result, these adults are inconsistent in discipline. They have a tendency to talk too much, nag without following through and give too many chances. Their children do not take them seriously, because they do not say what they mean or mean what they say.

Adults in the permissive by choice style tend to adopt the lose-lose stance toward conflict. No one's needs get met. While adults in the permissive by default style tend to adopt a lose-win conflict style (generally within this style the child wins and the adult loses, because the child holds the power in the relationship. With both styles, the question becomes: What cost are you willing to pay to protect the trust and respect in the relationship?

Children who experience this style may develop a pattern known as impulsive-aggressive. Some of the resultant traits may be: higher levels of impulsivity and aggressiveness, a quick temper, lacking appropriate self-control and self-reliance, lower levels of resourcefulness, social immaturity, a sense of confusion about authority, higher risk of alcohol and substance abuse, and lower levels of motivation.

Authoritative

Authoritative caregivers respond to situations and the behaviors of children in positive, effective and nurturing ways. This style is based on mutual respect. The rules are clear, reasonable and fair.

This style is high in demands and structure and high in responsiveness and nurturance. These adults solicit and consider the ideas, emotions and opinions of children. There are give-and-take discussions. The communication style is open, honest, responsive and clear. Children's emotions are acknowledged and validated. For example, "It is ok to be angry, but it is not ok to hurt others when you are angry." In this style, all emotions are valued, but boundaries are set around the behaviors the child uses to express emotions when their choices could potentially be hurtful or destructive. Authoritative adults teach children alternative behaviors. "Let's figure out another way for you to tell me that you are angry."

Authoritative adults use positive methods of discipline. These strategies include:

- Choices

- Natural Consequences

- Logical Consequences

- Encouragement

- Positive Recognition

- Problem Solving

- Active Listening

- Redirection

- Role Modeling

- Renewal Time

- Giving Effective Commands

- Reframing *No*

- Establishing a "firm but gentle" structure (Rules, Schedules and Routines)

- Using "I" Messages

In addition, these adults create a win-win power structure, so that the needs of the child and the needs of the adult are met. The result is trust and mutual respect.

This style promotes the growth of children who are generally seen as well-adjusted and happy. This style increases cooperation, self-esteem and positive attitudes.

CONTINUUM OF THE CAREGIVER STYLES

AUTHORITARIAN (HIGH STRUCTURE)	AUTHORITATIVE (BALANCE)	PERMISSIVE (HIGH SUPPORT)
"You get your butt over here and sit down before I smack you."	"Sit down, because you cannot run in the store. I need your help."	Silence toward children, or "Ah, they're just kids."

In applying this continuum to our DISC model, it seems that the parents and educators who are a "D" or "C" type tend to gravitate toward an authoritarian style. They are structure experts. "I" and "S" type parents and educators gravitate toward a permissive style. They are the support experts.

$$D \qquad\qquad I$$
$$\swarrow \qquad\qquad\qquad \searrow$$
$$\leftarrow \text{AUTHORITARIAN} \rightarrow \text{AUTHORITATIVE} \leftarrow \text{PERMISSIVE} \rightarrow$$
$$\nwarrow \qquad\qquad\qquad \nearrow$$
$$C \qquad\qquad S$$

In order to develop the authoritative style (a balance of structure and support), the adult will have adjustments to make and skills to learn. This is known as "adjusting the fit." In other words, we can choose to manage our own styles. And, when we do, there are more possible outcomes.

For homes in which the two parents have a conflicting idea about parenting style, it is important for the two parents to make a conscious effort to blend their ideas into a system that is going to work in their home. It creates problems in a child's life if each parent is parenting in a different way.

ADJUSTING OUR FIT [32]

To become more balanced in our approach, each type may need to learn new skills or adjust their behaviors in the following ways:

"D" types may need to consider:

- Giving choices, whenever possible.
- Showing affection toward others - saying *I love you*, giving hugs and kisses, and verbalizing positive emotions.
- Taking time away from tasks to have fun and enjoy the relationship - spending quality time with others.
- Actively listening - listening for understanding.
- Being more patient.
- Compromising - others have ideas and opinions to share. Avoid being too opinionated.
- Being more sensitive to the feelings of others - avoid sarcasm and harsh communication.

"I" types may need to consider:

- Developing consistency.
- Setting clear limits.
- Actively listening and talking less.
- Following through on discipline - taking a firm stand.
- Staying focused on the task at hand.
- Slowing down the pace and reducing emotional expressions.
- Giving warnings when things are about to change - reduce spontaneity.
- Focusing on prioritizing and keeping commitments.
- Staying out of persistent and persuasive arguments.

"S" types may need to consider:

- Speaking up when upset rather than bottling up their feelings.

- Getting outside your comfort zone and taking some risks.

- Becoming more decisive - *no* means *no*. Be firm.

- Accepting conflict as an inevitable part of life.

- Letting a child experience the consequences of his actions - avoid becoming a rescuer.

- Planning one thing per week to take care of yourself.

- Trying not to solve everyone's problems and make everyone happy - avoid over-accommodation.

"C" types may need to consider:

- Modifying their "perfectionistic" view and encourage a child's growth according to her pattern, not yours.

- Guarding against over-explaining and boring others with details.

- Ensuring that schedules and tasks do not become more important than relationships and relaxing.

- Becoming more spontaneous - lighten up!

- Becoming more flexible. There is more than one way to get to the end result.

- Allowing risk-taking within the parameters of wisdom and safety.

- Explaining step-by-step how you want something done – verbalizing ideas more fully - others cannot read your mind.

- Avoiding questions – reduce the amount of questions. It feels like interrogation to many children. Interrogation stops communication.

- Allowing "undirected activities." This means there is time to do nothing (daydreaming, sleeping, chillin').

PROGRAMMATIC ENVIRONMENT

As we connect the environment to the DISC model, it is clear that different types require different environmental characteristics.

"D" children seek an environment that recognizes them for their capabilities and leadership potential. They respond to adults who provide direct, bottom-line answers and allow freedom for individual achievement. It is wise for adults to give them choices as many times as possible. For example: "You can choose to go to bed anytime before 10:00 – but the latest is 10:00." In addition, "Ds" thrive on competition and persist toward their goal. Once an idea enters their head, it stays there until it is accomplished. It is not likely they will become flexible in their thinking, but rather invest all of their energies into getting you to change your thinking. To a "D", everything is either black or white. There is no gray area. These children are self-sufficient. They prefer varied and challenging activities. When things stay the same too long, "D" types get bored. This boredom can lead "Ds" to challenge you in ways you wish they wouldn't. They experience greater levels of success when the environment provides them opportunities to move, act and do. "D" children may not show a preference toward reading or talking about something. They just want to get right to it. These children prefer physical education classes, recess, studying business, debating, going on field trips and constructing things. As they consider their future, "D" types may want to know that they have a natural giftedness for business, athletics, military service, law, law enforcement, medicine, construction and mechanics.*

It is important to make healthy adjustments to meet the needs of every child. If adults neglect to do this, they will find that they need to deal with destructive or disruptive behaviors in that child.

"I" children seek an environment that has lots of activity and contact with friendly people. They respond to an adult who provides them with attention and offers positive affirmation and affection. When talking with an "I" child, it is helpful to be expressive and use stories to emphasize your point. For example, when the children did not pick up the dolls in the dramatic play area, the teacher left a note that said, "We felt sad all night, because we had to sleep on the floor, and we were cold. We hope you take care of us today. Please put us in the cradle, and cover us with a blanket before you go home. Thanks, the dolls." It is also beneficial to have this child repeat back what you have said to ensure the message was delivered. There are times when "I" children do not stop talking long enough to listen and hear what is being said. Enthusiasm and optimism are two of their greatest character traits, and they respect a leader who provides both. "I" children experience greater levels of success on short-term projects. They prefer activities that are entertaining and relevant to their life experiences. Hands-on experiences and unscheduled times for fun are critical to an "I's" well-being. Like the "Ds", these children like to move and act. However, they prefer talking about doing something and inspiring others to do it, rather than getting it done themselves. "I" type children incorporate feelings into everything they do and want you to do the same. These children prefer group activities that involve discussion and sharing opinions. They generally embrace cooperative learning, oral presentations, storytelling and reading out loud. They have a flair for the dramatic and are imaginative and therefore, enjoy theater, acting and role-playing. As they consider their future, "I" children may want to know that they have a natural giftedness toward composing, designing, sales, communications, entertainment, politics and public speaking.*

"S" type children seek an environment that is consistent, predictable and familiar. These children respond best to an adult who is relaxed and displays a quiet, gentle strength. When talking with an "S" child, it is helpful to be soft-spoken and patient. Expressing appreciation for their contributions will work wonders. "S" children like to hear the message, "I would really appreciate your help," instead of, "You need to help right now!" "D" children positively respond to the message, "Different choices, different results. If you don't like the results you got, make a different choice." With "S" children, this message is too harsh and direct. They may respond to those words by crying and asking, "Why are you yelling at me?" In addition, "S" type children experience greater levels of success when the adult clearly defines the goal and then provides them with all the information and means needed to reach the goal. "Ss" enjoy working in a group, but they prefer interaction with only two to four children. "S" children prefer quiet activities and at times, want to be alone. Therefore, providing spaces for escape and privacy are critical to their well-being. Children of this type seem to embrace writing, reading, listening to music, enjoying nature and doing crafts. As they consider their future, "S" children may want to know that they have a natural giftedness toward service professions such as counseling, teaching, nursing, social work, real estate agents, managers and librarians.*

"C" children seek an environment that has clearly-defined tasks and sufficient time and resources to accomplish the tasks. The environment needs to be clean and organized. They appreciate an adult who minimizes risk and maintains a supportive climate. Structure through schedules and routines are critical to their well-being. They do not like surprises. "C" children like an adult that is reasonable and fair. When talking with them, it is helpful to provide detailed information. They tend to be literal in their communication. For example, while sitting at a morning meeting, Kyle was told to "zip his lips." Many children would understand that this means to be quiet. Kyle, however, leaned back and attempted to put the zipper on his pants to his lips. In doing so, he fell backward and was asked to leave the meeting. Now, that's an example of literal communication! "C" children experience greater levels of success when they are given uninterrupted time to work independently. They tend to embrace formulas and theories, intellectual ideas, opportunities to question and experiment, and chances to conduct research. They have a private style. As they consider their future, "C" children may want to know that they have a natural giftedness toward mathematics, computer technology, philosophy, medicine, engineering, photography, teaching and architecture.*

THE PHILOSOPHICAL ENVIRONMENT

The philosophical environment is about the beliefs we hold about how children develop and learn and what and how they should be taught. For example, do we believe that it is in a child's best interest to do things for him, even when he is capable of doing things for himself? Or do we believe it is better to support him in his efforts to do things so he develops a sense of competence and develops initiative? Another controversial, yet important philosophical question is should we spank children? The answers to these types of questions and issues will guide and direct your daily interactions with children and the type of environment created for them.

---

* It is unwise to push or force a child into a career that seems right for him and his personality style. Any child can choose any career. The only downside is that the child may have to work against his natural tendencies and gifts in that career.

CHAPTER 9

BEYOND BOSSING, BEGGING AND BRIBING

"With every deed you are sowing a seed,
though the harvest you may never see."

Ella Wheeler Wilcox [33]

9

In your mind's eye, look ahead to the year when your child will be twenty-one years old. What traits or qualities do you hope to see? Is it your hope that she will be independent, responsible, respectful, popular or humorous? Now rewind the tape. You have a number of years to reach this picture. The choices you make each day will determine if and when the picture is achieved. We must acknowledge that positive guidance is the most effective road to travel toward this picture. Only through positive guidance can we teach self - regulation and self - control.

There are many negative statements that adults frequently use. Here are some examples:

"You'll do it, because I said so. I'm your father."

"What part of *no* don't you understand?"

"I tell you over and over again. When will you ever get it?"

"You should be ashamed of yourself."

All of these statements are given by adults in hopes that children will respond to their authority.

Diane

One day, I was working in an after-school program. A mom entered at 5:15 to pick up her daughter. Upon entering, she walked over to her daughter and said, "Diane, come on. Get your things. We have to get home and make supper, so I can get your brother to soccer practice on time."

Diane continued playing. Her mom repeated her instructions, but Diane did not budge. Her mom repeated herself a third time, but the results were the same. Diane continued playing. By the time the mom spoke the fourth time, it did not sound the same as the first few times. She was now begging. "Please, Diane, get your coat and backpack. If you do, we can stop at McDonald's on the way home. I would really appreciate your help."

Diane continued playing and said, "Just wait a few minutes. I'm almost done."

At this point, her mom was out of patience and time. She began speaking with great force in her voice, "Diane Rose, you better get your things right this minute, young lady. You wait until you get home. Your father is going to hear about this. Now get in that car as fast as you know how. Do you hear me? NOW!"

Ineffective Methods Produce Ineffective Results

This chapter has given examples of common, yet ineffective methods of getting children to respond to our influence. They are ineffective for several reasons. First, they do not teach the child what to do. Secondly, they do not address the child's behavior and what needs to change. Thirdly, some of the statements even attack the character of the child.

The long-term results of using these ineffective methods are all negative. The short-term results vary. Depending on the temperament of the child, some will change their behaviors temporarily, as long as the adult is present to instill fear. Then once the adult is gone, the behavior returns.

The previous examples were negative and will have negative consequences. It is important for adults to understand what is involved in positive guidance. Part of positive guidance is anticipating, and thus preventing, problems. One of the best ways to do this is by creating secure attached relationships with children.

Creating A Secure, Attached Relationship

I recommend that you evaluate your relationship with a child by cutting out a red heart from a piece of construction paper. This heart should be about nine inches across its mid-section. On the inside mid-section of the heart, write down all the things you do or say that make this child know he is loved unconditionally. On the outside edge of the heart, write down all the things you have said or done that left this child feeling unloved or less than good about himself. Now, rip off all the statements written on the outside edge, leaving only the mid-section of the heart. How big is this child's heart now?

There are times, as parents or educators, when we have done things unintentionally that have interfered with our relationship to a child. Picture a child like a balloon. Some children have a lot of helium inside, and we say their self-esteem is healthy. When the self-esteem is healthy, their behaviors seem to be healthier as well.

For this next illustration, you will need two inflated balloons, a sharp knife and a fork. Pick up one balloon. Now think back to your interactions with a particular child. Has there ever been a time when you said something and after you said it, you got this uneasy feeling? You immediately thought, "I shouldn't have said that. It's not what I meant. But the damage is done." Pick up the sharp knife and puncture the balloon. This is the effect of cutting words on the self-esteem of that child. Knowing we have wronged this child, we apologize. This may sound like, "I'm sorry. Please forgive me." We can begin to repair the shattered spirit by apologizing.

It is important to remember that cutting words produce emotionally bleeding hearts. You may be thinking that you do not use cutting words. So let me briefly give an example of cutting words. When we publicly and continually refer to the "S" child as "shy," we deliver the message that this must be his or her destiny. Thus, "S" children cannot and should not learn assertiveness. In addition, when we refer to the "D" child as stubborn, we deliver the message that persistence is not valued. Your words may become a self-fulfilling prophecy.

Now pick up the second balloon. Again think back to your interactions with a particular child. Has there ever been a time when this child has misread your seriousness and intense look? I have. I will share one example. When my daughter was four years old, she asked me why I was always mad at her. I stated that I wasn't mad, but she insisted I was. I asked her why she thought I was mad, and she told me to go look at my face. For the first time, I realized I had a scowl on my face that showed as a furrowed brow and deep lines vertically between my eyes. I also realized that I had this look when I was tired or busy.

Next, take the fork and pierce the balloon. To Erin, this look was a piercing look that she interpreted as anger. Over time, this look had a negative effect on her self-esteem. In order for Erin to understand this look, I taught her to ask me if I was tired or busy whenever she saw it on my face. To this day, Erin, and my other children, will ask, "Mom, are you tired?"

I will add emphasis to this point by using a story about the balloon man at the parade: A young boy approaches the balloon man and asks him, "What happens when you let go of the red balloon?" The balloon man releases the red balloon, and it soars. The young child then asks, "What happens when you let go of the green balloon?" Again, the balloon man releases the balloon, and it rises. A third time, the young lad asks, "What happens when you let go of the orange balloon?" And as would be expected, it rises. The young child does not understand, so he asks, "How come they all go up in the air?"

The balloon man answers, "Son, it's not the color of the balloon that matters. It's what's inside that counts."

This is true with children. There are some children who have a healthy self-esteem and secure attached relationships. These children, once released, soar to heights unseen by the naked eye. They by-pass or overcome all the obstacles in life. There are other children who have enough inside to begin to soar, but get caught up in the trees and telephone lines of life. All these children need is one adult with enough courage and wisdom to release them from their obstacles, so they can soar once more. A third group of children are released and are soon found depleted of the inner stuff and are seen sadly bouncing along the floor of life. These children need one adult who will fill them up again through encouragement. Once this is done, these children will soar one more day.

Concluding thoughts

Children enter this world, and your environment, not knowing who they are, and they learn this through their interactions with significant people in their life. Adults act like a mirror. Through the words and actions of adults, children see a reflection of themselves. These reflections become what they believe about themselves. Therefore, adults have a choice to reflect rejection or acceptance, approval or disapproval. Whatever our choice, we will have a powerful influence on each child that has a relationship with us.

One question I have asked many parents over the years is, "If you treated your friends as you treat your children, how many friends would you have?" This is not to imply that children and adults are equal on all matters, but on those related to human dignity and respect, we should be equal.

CHAPTER 10

NO DISCONNECT HERE

"You must be able to say sincerely, the fact that we see things differently is a strength - not a weakness - in our relationship."

Stephen Covey[34]

10

B y now, we all know that our influence will have a lasting impression on a child's life. We have the ability to uplift a child's spirit or dash it with insensitivity. We have the capacity to empower their full potential or intimidate. We have the power to support or undermine their growth. We can choose to respond or react. I will add that we must use our influence wisely and this includes using positive guidance to address their behaviors.

Changing our view of and approach to children presents an overwhelming challenge, but it is critical to their success. Rather than suppress their emotions and behaviors, we will do better to guide them and empower children through their personality style. Rather than focus on the problems, we must shift to the solutions. Rather than control, we need to teach. Remember, our goal is not to break the spirit of the child, but to teach him how to work with his natural style.

As we think about how our view might change, take a pencil and a piece of paper. On this piece of paper, write down all that comes to your mind when you hear the word "discipline." This is a free association activity so do not censor or evaluate what you write. Just write whatever enters your frame of reference.

Now that this is complete, take a second piece of paper and draw two frames as illustrated on the next page.

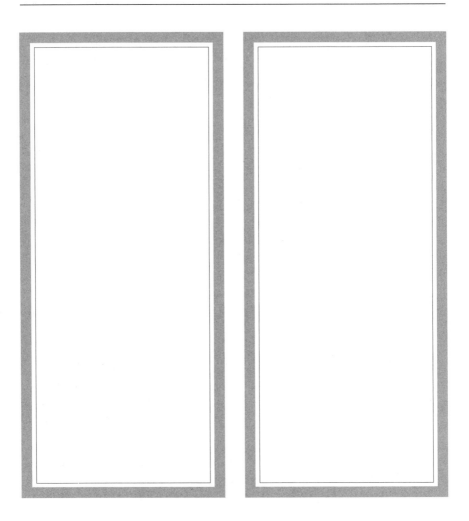

In the frame farthest to your left, write down all the things from your list that you would have wanted an adult to do when you were disciplined as a child. In the frame on the right, write those things from your list that you wished adults did not do when you were disciplined as a child.

This activity highlights the differing views on guiding behaviors of children. If I were to work with your child and her behaviors, which frame would you like me to work from? Note that for many children, the frame they experience is the right frame.

In many cases, positive improvement in a child's behavior will be produced through simply reframing the approach to discipline. Effective discipline can be seen as positive guidance. Adults must be able to set fair and reasonable limits for children. In doing so, I draw your attention to a concept called "the three-legged stool."

THE THREE-LEGGED STOOL

The seat of the stool is cut in a heart shape, because it represents the emotions and heart of the child. The three legs that are supporting the seat of the stool represent what we can and should do for this child. A child's sense of safety and stability is directly connected to our ability to do three things for him.

THE FIRST LEG OF THE STOOL

The first leg represents setting limits, rules and expectations for a child's behavior. As we tackle this task, it is vital to prioritize what is really important. In the field of behavior, safety holds the highest priority. Here is an example of expressing a limit that emphasizes safety, "Put your seatbelt on when we are riding in the car."

A second consideration in establishing limits is to understand that a few rules followed are better than many rules not followed. To illustrate this point, I will use another story about a child named Bryan.

Bryan

Bryan was four years old, and his IQ was tested to be 148. This places him well above average in the range of intelligence testing. His mother was a high "C" (Careful/Cautious temperament). Bryan was a high "I" (Inspiring/Influencing temperament). Bryan's dad was a high "S" (Supportive/Sweet temperament).

I asked Bryan's mom to write down all the rules she had for Bryan to follow in her home. Seven days later, she returned the list. It filled six notebook pages of paper on both sides. I asked Bryan's dad to do the same. Two days later, I had his list of twelve rules. I then, asked Bryan to tell me all the rules he had in his house. Bryan grinned and said, "That's easy. You can't put your feet on the table when you're eating, and you gotta wear your seatbelt." I compared what Bryan told me to the lists from his parents. Bryan's two rules were not included anywhere on his mom's six pages of rules. The seatbelt rule was written on his dad's list.

The mom's list was a typical high "C" list. The expectations were high, and compliance and conformity to the rules were demanded. In addition, mom thought that because his IQ was so high, he should be able to learn all that was expected. However, Bryan was a high "I" and structure and rules were not his priority. No matter how smart he was, he was not going to respond positively to the procedures and standards of his mother. (In general, average four-year-old children can internalize and respond to three to five rules.)

Rules need to be stated positively.

The rules Bryan's mom had were written in the negative: "No jumping on the beds; no talking with food in your mouth; no hitting your brother; no splashing water in the bathtub; and no running in the house." While these told Bryan what he could not do, they did not teach him what to do. Stated positively, these rules would have been written, "We jump outside or on a trampoline; we swallow our food before talking; we keep our hands to ourselves unless someone tells you that you can touch him; we keep the water in the bathtub so no one slips on the wet floor; and we run in the yard.

THE SECOND LEG OF THE STOOL

The second leg of the stool represents consequences to the rules. The consequences you establish are influenced by your past experiences, your cultural and ethnic background, and your values and beliefs. The consequences you use form your discipline technique. The word "discipline" comes from *disciple*, which means to follow and learn. Therefore, the process of discipline is to teach, so that our children can follow and learn.

Dennis

Dennis is a six-year-old who refuses to eat what is prepared for dinner. During dinner, he whines and pouts for something else to eat. His parents realize that Dennis has a choice about whether he will eat or not, but they do not choose to listen to his whining. He is required to leave the table until he can sit and eat without whining. His dinner remains on the table at his place until the mealtime is over. At any point during the mealtime, he can return to the table and eat his dinner. However, should Dennis choose not to eat and the mealtime has ended, his plate is removed, and Dennis will not be served any food until the next meal. Therefore, if Dennis does not eat, his consequences are the feelings of hunger that he experiences.

THE THIRD LEG OF THE STOOL

Once the consequences are established, we can explore the third leg of "the three-legged stool." This leg represents the follow - through on the consequences. Our follow - through must be timely and consistent, and in many cases, this may not mean convenient. A child's sense of safety and security does not wait until all our ducks are in a row and all the conditions are to our liking. Children continue to grow and learn through every interaction or lack of interaction.

When our follow - through is inconsistent, nonexistent or harsh, children will learn to play "kid's lottery." This means they will seek out the adult who is inconsistent or nonexistent in their follow - through and avoid the adult who is consistent or harsh. In following through, "S" and "I" type adults appear to lean toward inconsistent or nonexistent, while "D" and "C" types lean toward being consistent or harsh. For example, a "D" little girl learns that persistently demanding from an "S" or "I" parent will probably net the results she was after. An "I" little boy learns that falling at the feet of an "S" or "I" parent, while putting on a sad, puppy-dog face and promising the moon, may net the results he was seeking. For example, "Please Mom! I promise I'll never do it again. I promise. I love you, Mom. You're the best mom in the whole world. I'm going to marry you one day."

Moreover, when a parent is inconsistent, the child learns that *no* does not mean *no*. He learns to just keep asking. The child comes to realize that there is a 50-50 chance of getting the desired result.

Punishment

Punishment is a particular type of follow - through consequence. For example, in referring back to the example of Dennis and his refusal to eat, a punishment follow-through consequence would be sending Dennis to stand in the corner or sending him to bed early. This type of consequence is not usually a recommended approach, because it undermines the dignity of the child.

Concluding Comments on The Three-Legged Stool

As you may imagine, when we remove any one of the legs from the underside of the stool, the seat (representing the heart of the child) crashes. And, the question remains: Is this what we are trying to do in our role of parenting and educating children? If not, then what will we commit to doing differently?

CHAPTER 11

POSITIVE DISCIPLINE

"Most children need discipline. Dealing with disobedient and disruptive students can be challenging… Discipline must be motivating. All children have "hot buttons" that ignite them. Students also have "cold buttons" that turn them off. A teacher's personal "hot button" can be a certain student's "cold button." In other words, things that motivate the teacher may, in fact, do just the opposite for a student."

Dr. Robert Rohm [35]

11

Providing positive discipline is a huge component in gaining the best short-term and long-term results with children. This type of discipline also aids in the maturing process of children.

Positive Discipline Strategies

- Adding Choices
- Effective Commands
- Reframing *No*
- You are Powerful When...
- Active Listening
- Praise
- Encouragement
- Positive Problem-Solving

ADDING CHOICES

Adding choices is very important. In this strategy, an adult can present two or three viable options, and let the child decide what he or she will do. Simple choices are generally "either - or" in nature. For example, "Kathy, you can do _____ or _____ . What's your choice?"

Typically, we would use simple choices with young children,

between the ages of 2 to 6 years, or with older children who do not have the experience or comfort with making choices. Multiple choices add more than two options. For example, "Kathy, you can do _____ , _____ or _____ . What's your choice?"

Multiple choices are used with older children, between the ages of 7-10 years or with younger children who are capable of handling them. When children reach the middle years, between the ages of 10-15 years, we ask for a few possible choices from them, and we can talk about them and negotiate: "Kathy, what have you considered? Come up with two or three ideas, and we'll talk about them." By adolescence, wise choices are made independently, because you have invested your time into the teaching process.

While offering choices is important for all children, this strategy takes on increased importance when working with a "D" type child. This child has a need for control and may be predisposed toward defiance and power-based behaviors. Offering choices allows the child to maintain a sense of control within parameters and power struggles are minimized. Nevertheless, do not be naïve and think this is a magic wand. With a "D" child, it is predictable that offering choices leads to her trying to test the limit through re-negotiation or she may just stare at you in silence. If the choice is about bedtime, you can say, "You can go to bed anytime between now and 9:00, but 9:00 is the latest."

Once you set a boundary, do not negotiate. "D" children like to be in control, and they will frequently place new options on the table. Be firm and continue to present the same options. When the child does not choose from the options presented, you may want to say, "I have given you the choices. You may choose from one of those options. If you continue to try to get me to change, I will make the decision for you." If the child continues to try to change the options, the parent may say, "It looks like you are not ready to make choices in this area. So this time, I will make it for you. Next time, you'll get another chance."

EFFECTIVE COMMANDS

How do you communicate with a child so that he or she hears your direction and initiates an appropriate response? The answer is effective commands.

According to current research, when working with children who have a pattern of defiance, there are often significant improvements in their level of responsiveness when the adult gives effective commands. Effective commands enable the child to understand the message and the seriousness of the message.

When you are working with a "D" child or any child who does not respond to adult authority, it is strongly recommended that you do the following:

- *Make sure you mean what you are about to say.* If you do not mean it, then do not say it. Once said, it is essential that you follow through to completion.

- *State the command simply, directly and in a matter-of-fact tone of voice.* "It is time to get your coat on." It is most effective when the command has a period as the punctuation at the end. Do not present it as a question, suggestion or favor.

- *Give one command at a time. "Pajamas, Now."* Too often, the command gets lost in a barrage of words. For example, "David, pick up your toys, get your pajamas on, brush your teeth, then turn off the light and get into bed. Did you hear me? Hop to it, young man!" Most young children can only follow one-step commands. In the example previously given, there are five commands.

- *Give the command from a distance of 3 to 5 feet from the child.* This delivers the message to the child that you intend on following through to completion, and you expect him to respond. Often times, we are watching television in the family room, and the child is playing in another room. We yell the command from one room to the next or up a flight of stairs. Fifteen minutes later, we yell, "I'm coming up there. You better be doing what I asked." And when the television show is over, we walk up the stairs to follow through, but thirty minutes or more has passed.

- *Consistency of follow - through is the key.* It is through consistency that children learn that what you say is what you mean. I have told many a child, "You can test me if you want, but in my book no means no."

- *When commands are responded to, positive consequences must follow.* The child may receive a positive comment like "thanks," or "I appreciate your cooperation. Cooperating is powerful."

- *When commands are not responded to, negative consequences must follow.* When the child does not go to bed, an earlier bedtime tomorrow follows.

REFRAMING *NO*

Reframing *No* is a helpful strategy to use. When working with a "D" child, there are certain words that trigger the competitive and powerful nature of this child. These words are "no, stop, don't, can't and wait." When he hears the word "no," he begins to think, "Oh yes, I can!" When he hears the word "stop," he may increase the action. When he hears the word "can't," he thinks, "I'll show you. Watch me!" Therefore, these words are reserved for times of great importance or safety. To reframe *no*, you may want to choose one of these alternatives:

- *Give the child information but leave out the NO.* The child asks, "Can I watch this video?"

  Instead of saying *no*, say, "That's not a video for children."

- *Accept the child's feelings.* The child says, "I don't want to leave yet. I'm still playing."

  Instead of saying, "We can't stay any longer," the adult might say, "I can see it's hard for you to leave when you're having fun, but it's time to go now."

- *Describe the problem.* The child asks, "Can you take me over to Patti's house now?"

  Instead of saying, "No, not now; can't you see that I'm busy?" you might say, "I'd like to help you out, but I'm waiting for a call from the cable company."

- *When possible, substitute a yes for a no:* The child asks, "Can we go to the playground?

  Instead of saying, "No, we have to eat lunch first," we might say, "Yes, right after lunch."

- *Give yourself time to think.* The child asks, "Can I get this?"

  Instead of saying *no*, you might say, "I'll bet you would love to have it. Let me think about it."

YOU ARE POWERFUL WHEN...

It is a fact that all individuals want a sense of power and control over their life, and children are no exception. There is a strategy that teaches children how to gain that sense of power. It is called YOU ARE POWERFUL WHEN. This is the starter phrase, and we add an ending such as...

You are Powerful When You...

- Help Someone
- Make a New Friend
- Compliment Others
- Use Please and Thank You
- Listen When Others Talk*

*Note that you may choose to add any other ending that is appropriate to the skills you are trying to teach the child. The ultimate goal is to bring the child power in his or her relationships and life.

ACTIVE LISTENING

Active listening is an effective way to solicit a child's emotions and open the communication. The adult acts as a mirror and reflects back to the child what he is saying, while clarifying the message and the feelings conveyed through the words and nonverbal communication. This is far more helpful than telling a child how he should or should not feel, because active listening leads to solutions. The goal is for the child to know he was heard, and so he feels understood.

During active listening, the adult is to:

- Listen to the child's message, understand what the message means and what the child may be feeling. For example, "I hate you! I'm going to live with Grandma." The emotion expressed is anger.

- Put the understanding of the message into her own words and feed it back to the child for verification. "I think what I'm hearing you say is that I did something that made you feel angry."

- Suspend judgment and avoid lecturing. Do not try to persuade the child to feel differently or defend your position. For example, "It is ok if you feel angry with me. I'm your mother, and I love you."

- Validate the child's emotions. "It's ok to be angry with what I did, but now let's figure out what we can do to work this out."

Active Listening Openers

You think…

You seem…

It sounds to me like…

We agree on…

What you are trying to tell me is…

What's important to you right now is…

As you see things…

Let me see if I understand…

So you seem to be feeling…

Let me repeat what I heard…

So you would like me to…

PRAISE

Praise is defined as the positive descriptions we give for desirable behavior. It is a way to offer recognition and approval for a job well done. The goal is to comment on these positive behaviors throughout the day. This is known as "catch 'em being good."

Praise may be non-descriptive or descriptive, verbal or nonverbal. Non-descriptive praise sounds like, "Terrific!" or "Awesome!" These let the child know something she did met with your approval, but she has no way of knowing what she did to earn the comment. Descriptive praise specifies exactly what this child did to earn the approval or recognition from the adult. It may sound like, "I like the way you cleaned your room by putting all the toys on the shelves neatly. That was awesome."

Verbal praise, as its name implies, means using words to comment about the child's behavior. Nonverbal praise uses body language, such as a nod of the head, a smile, a wink, a thumbs-up hand gesture or an A-OK hand signal.

When using praise with children, it is recommended to combine descriptive, verbal praise with nonverbal praise. (This gives a child positive recognition.) This is because most communication happens through body language, according to those who have studied this field extensively. In addition, there may be times when you are not close enough to the child to speak to him, but you can catch his eye and gesture the message of approval.

Soggy Potato Chip Theory

At this juncture, I would like to share another concept known as the "soggy potato chip theory." This theory is based on the idea that if a child is offered a choice between a nice crisp potato chip and a soggy potato chip, he will choose the better chip. However, when a child is offered the choice between getting something, even a soggy potato chip or getting nothing (no potato chip at all), the child will choose the soggy potato chip. The analogy of the potato chip directly connects to the use of positive attention, negative attention or being ignored. When there is a choice between positive attention (crisp potato chip) and negative attention (soggy potato chip), a child prefers and chooses the positive. But when given a choice between negative attention and being ignored (no potato chip at all), the child chooses negative attention.

What this analogy has done is create for you a new association to potato chips. The hope is that the next time you see, hold or eat chips, you will think about what kind of chip you have been in the lives of children. The balance is providing fourteen times more positive than negative.

Praise the Sticks

Over the years, we have used a strategy called Praise the Sticks. This has been implemented as part of a family or class meetings. In this activity, each person has a name tag, similar to the one you receive at a conference. The tag says, "Hello my name is." As the meeting begins, each person sitting at the meeting must state one compliment about each participant in the group. As these statements are voiced, a recorder writes them onto that participant's tag. When there are twenty children in the meeting, each child leaves that meeting with a tag listing nineteen comments about himself or herself.

When praise is overused, it can lead to a false sense of self-esteem. Therefore, it is important to use it in balance with encouragement. It is recommended that there be four times more encouragement used than praise.

ENCOURAGEMENT

The word "encouragement" means to inspire courage. When used as a guidance strategy, encouragement means being specific about the child's efforts and the progress she is making, rather than the finished result. It is nonjudgmental.

Encouragement communicates, "I am with you; I care; I want to help."

Encouragement Openers

Let's try it together.

I'm sure you can straighten this out, but if you need help you know where I am.

I understand, some days are harder than others...

I know it is hard, but I think you can handle this.

Want to try?

When you are ready, we'll get started...

Let's start over. This time will be better.

I believe in you.

You have great potential.

Your best days are ahead of you.

Audiotapes

To check whether we are in balance, I challenge you to have someone audiotape while you are in the presence of children. Once the tape is completed, this individual will hand you the tape, and you will listen to it in the privacy of your car or home. What you will be listening for is whose voice dominates the tape, the number of times praise is used, the number of times encouragement is used and your tone of voice. From this tape, it will become clear the areas of strength in your style and those that need enhancement.

POSITIVE PROBLEM-SOLVING

Problem-solving is a strategy that taps into the natural giftedness of critical thinking associated with the "C" type child. According to Elizabeth Crary, an expert on children's problem-solving, "The primary job of the adult facilitator is to help the child remain focused on the problem and the problem - solving process."[36]

Developing a problem-solving strategy can help adults to logically and easily move from a problem to a solution. Here are the steps that I suggest you consider when you are faced with a difficult problem.

Steps to Problem-Solving

- Define the Problem
- Identify the Expectation
- Brainstorming
- Evaluate the Alternatives
- Planning
- Implementation
- Evaluate the Implementation

The steps of problem-solving will be explained as you read the next example that deals with a boy named Matthew.

Matthew

Matthew was a four - year - old child diagnosed with Bipolar Disorder and Obsessive Compulsive Disorder. One day, Matthew's teacher called me out of a meeting. There was a sense of urgency in her voice. As I quickly walked with her toward the children's bathroom, it became obvious that Matthew was in the bathroom. As we opened the door to the bathroom, we saw Matthew pacing back and forth while stating, "I'm not listening to no stupid a__hole teacher." With each pass, he repeated this statement.

Define the Problem

I immediately put Matthew into the first step of the problem-solving approach which is "defining the problem." I asked him, "Matthew, what's the problem?"

Matthew angrily replied, "I told you, I'm not listening to no..." I stopped him from continuing any further. I turned to his teacher and asked how long he had been doing this behavior. Her answer was twenty minutes.

I then inquired about her plan for working with Matthew, and she responded, "I did it - I went to get you."

Turning my attention back to Matthew, I again wanted to define the problem. I asked Matthew, "Where are you right now?"

He replied, "In the bathroom."

"And where are you supposed to be right now?"

"In my classroom resting, but I don't rest."

"So Matthew, you are supposed to be in your classroom quiet, but instead you are in the bathroom swearing at your teacher?"

"Yes."

"Well, Matthew, that's the problem."

(Now, the problem has been defined and clearly stated.)

Identify the Expectation

As the process continued, I identified the expectation. "Matthew, tomorrow at rest time, you will stay in your classroom. You will be quiet, so that the children who want to sleep can do so. You do not have to sleep, but you do have to stay quiet. So what are you going to do to make sure this happens?" (Matthew is now entering the next step of the problem-solving approach known as brainstorming or generating ideas.)

Brainstorming

Matthew asked if I had a piece of paper and a pencil. I said *yes*. He then directed me to write down number 1 and circle it. Having done so, I asked what I should write next. Matthew told me to write the word "chess."

"Matthew, do you know how to play chess?" He nodded *yes*. "Well, I don't, but I can learn if you'll teach me." (This response shifted the power to Matthew.)

"Matthew, if we didn't pick that one, what would you pick next?" He then instructed me to write down number 2 and circle it. "Ok, what is it?"

"Checkers."

"You know how to play checkers, too?" Again, Matthew nodded. "I do too, so don't pick it, because you'll lose." (The power has shifted back into my court.)

"So if you don't want to lose, Matthew, what would you pick next?" The young boy then shared with me that the third choice would be a Rubik's cube.

At this point, I started to laugh. Matthew got angry and said, "Don't laugh at me!" I explained to him that I was not laughing at him, but at the fact that we did not have chess, checkers or a Rubik's cube in the classroom.

Matthew smiled and said, "And, that's the problem!"

As we continued with the brainstorming, Matthew said that number 4 was brain teasers, and number 5 was a computer.

There was a computer in the classroom, and I confronted Matthew with that fact. "Matthew, we have a computer, so what's the deal?"

He replied, "Not the baby games."

"What games are you looking for then?"

"Blackjack."

Evaluate the Alternatives

Matthew was satisfied with five alternatives. The next step was to evaluate these alternatives. Matthew and I discussed each of the five alternatives, and he chose checkers as the best one to try first. He then assured me that he would stay in his classroom and be quiet during rest time.

Planning

We then talked about the materials that we would need. I assured Matthew that I would provide a checkers game. Then we went over the expectations. (It was important to settle on who would have the red checkers and who would have the first move.)

Implementation

The following day, we played checkers at rest time, and Matthew was quiet in the process. When we were done, I asked him how that worked for him. He said it was good.

"What are we going to do tomorrow?"

"Chess."

Evaluate Implementation

The evaluation of the implementation is the final step to the process. In this case, implementation went smoothly. The teacher stopped experiencing problems with Matthew during rest time. Thus, the process continued successfully.

Problem-Solving Questions

What could you do differently next time?

What other way could you have let me know that?

What other way could you could have handled this situation?

Next time, what are some of the things you might think about?

What helped you the most this time?

Did that work for you?

How can we work together to make this better for both of us?

The following chart will help you to more easily see the strategies that are preferred by each personality style.

Review of DISC and Positive Discipline Strategies

D	I
Choices	Praise
Effective Commands	Active Listening
Reframing *No*	
You Are Powerful When	

C	S
Problem-Solving	Encouragement

This chapter has given you some of the tools available to you to help you work with children. I hope they will be helpful, and that they inspired your imagination.

CHAPTER 12

DISC OR DIAGNOSIS?

"A young boy walks up to a philosopher and says, 'Master, I want knowledge.' The philosopher replies, 'How much do you want knowledge?' The boy answers, 'Oh, I really want it.'
'Well, to get knowledge you have to want it as you want nothing else. Just come with me.'
He took the boy to the seashore, where together they waded out until they were in water up to the boy's chin. Then the philosopher put his hand on the boy's shoulder and pushed him under the water. For a long moment, he held him there, kicking and squirming and struggling to be released. Finally, just before the drowning point, he let him up.
Back on the beach, the philosopher asked, 'When you were under water, what did you want more than anything else in the world?'
'Master, the thing I wanted more than anything else was air.' The philosopher replied, 'Well, when you want knowledge as you then wanted air, you will get knowledge.'"

Author Unknown

12

While I would never recommend holding someone underwater to teach that person a lesson, the story you just read does make an excellent point. All of us have been underwater, and at that point, our main concern was getting air.

For the past fifty years, the field of mental health has been focused on labeling deficits, weaknesses or "illnesses" in children and adults, and treating those labels. Too often the focus has been on the attained results from an evaluation tool, rather than on the threats to the child's safety and dignity found as we observed his play and interactions with his environment. And, too often the parents have been blamed for being too strict or too lenient, too involved and overprotective, or too detached. But as Albert Einstein said, "The significant problems we face cannot be solved at the same level of thinking we were at when we created them."

Throughout the past fifty years or more, the *Diagnostic and Statistical Manual of Mental Disorders* has been used by psychologists, therapists, counselors and psychiatrists to define illnesses and provide labels. While those diagnoses do exist, there appears to be overlap in the criteria listed and the temperament traits identified in the DISC model. For example, a child with Attention Deficit Disorder with Hyperactivity, predominantly Hyperactive-Impulsive type, will have six or more of the following symptoms that have persisted for at least 6 months:

- Often fidgets with hands or feet or squirms in seat

- Often leaves seat in the classroom or in other situations in which remaining seated is expected

- Often runs about and climbs excessively in situations in which it is inappropriate

- Often has difficulty playing or engaging in leisure activities quietly

- Is often "on the go" or often acts as if "driven by a motor"

- Often talks excessively

- Often blurts out answers before questions have been completed

- Often has difficulty waiting for a turn

- Often interrupts or intrudes on others[37]

Note that these symptoms are also descriptive of a child with a high "I" temperament in the out-of-control mode.

A child diagnosed with Oppositional Defiant Disorder displays a pattern of negativistic, hostile and defiant behavior lasting at least six months, during which four (or more) of the following are present:

- Often loses temper

- Often argues with adults

- Often actively defies or refuses to comply with adult's requests or rules

- Often deliberately annoys people

- Often blames others for his or her mistakes or misbehavior

- Is often touchy or easily annoyed by others

- Is often angry and resentful

- Is often spiteful or vindictive[38]

These symptoms are also descriptive of a child with a high "D" temperament in the out-of-control mode.

Children with an "I/C" blend are the most emotionally expressive and sensitive. These children display broad mood swings. But does this mean the child should be diagnosed with Bipolar Disorder? Children with the "C/S" blend experience anxiety when they are separated from their parent, but does this warrant diagnosis of Separation Anxiety Disorder?

The answer is probably not, but it does highlight the fact that children of any temperament type or blend can develop challenging patterns of behaviors. However, those most likely to exhibit these behaviors are ones who are experiencing stress related to poorness of fit with their environment, or their needs are not met in a consistent, sensitive fashion, or they lack opportunities to practice and master the social-emotional tasks that underlie emotional wellness.

It is true that temperament traits can fall anywhere on a spectrum from healthy development to disturbance. For example, defiance is defined as repeated failure of a child to follow rules and respond positively to directions or requests. This spectrum begins in the toddler years and serves as a "declaration of independence." This is characterized by "no" to requests, limits or anything offered. This resistance develops early in the second year and lasts approximately six months. By the age of three, 90-95% of children are becoming more cooperative. Perhaps those not moving to a more cooperative posture are the 10% of children with the high "D" temperament.

When the behavior is developmental or caused by temperament, it does not warrant a diagnostic label. Instead, we may choose to:

- Realize this toddler has a need to control something, and therefore, we choose our battles wisely.

- Avoid power struggles.

- Give choices within parameters.

- Create predictability - rules, rituals and routines - for the times when the resistance is most likely to occur.

- Minimize the use of the words "no, stop, don't, can't and wait."

- Keep your intensity low by using a calm, neutral tone of voice. Avoid yelling, hovering over, over-controlling and nagging.

- Recognize all cooperative actions.

Noncompliance

As children move into the preschool years, the defiance may take the form of noncompliance. This type is defined as failure to initiate an appropriate response to adult directions within a 10-15 second period of its presentation. Since the behavior in the 3-6 year age group has been found to correlate to noncompliance throughout the lifespan and there is clear relationship with other behaviors (particularly tantrums and destructiveness), supportive interventions may be warranted. But at this point, diagnostic labeling is not valid. Instead, we must assess our parenting or teaching pattern.

According to the research, there are six parenting patterns that contribute to defiant responses from children.

- *Over-involvement in the life of the child.* Some children are showered with exaggerated attention and the child does not do for himself those things he is capable of doing or should be doing for himself, in order to grow in healthy ways. Instead, the adult shelters him from any perceived challenge.

- *An environment in which a constant state of happiness is the goal.* Some children live in an environment that shields them from all frustration and difficulties. The parent becomes the child's playmate and entertainment agent, ensuring that the child is occupied and content at all times.

- *Providing excessive shielding from risks.* This caregiver may say, "Don't go outside without your hat. You will catch a cold." When the reality is that colds come from a virus, not from going outside without a hat on your head. Then the child attempts to climb a tree, he hears, "Don't climb that tree. You'll fall and break your neck." Although this is a possibility, it does not happen to the majority of children climbing trees. And, the truth of the matter is that climbing trees can be fun, and it develops muscles.

- *Hypervigilance.* The adult has a preoccupation with the child's whereabouts and well-being. The caregiver is in a constant state of alert, and the child hears, "Stay close to me at all times. Someone could steal you!" In today's world, this happens, but children need a sense of freedom, within reason.

- *Nagging.* The adult gives an endless stream of directions, orders, commands, reminders, lectures and advice to the child. When this stream continues over time, the child sets up power struggles that show up as passive resistance or passive-aggressive behaviors.

- *Dejuvenilizing.* The adult treats the child as a substitute adult in order to obtain closeness, companionship and emotional intimacy.

For defiant responses, change the parenting pattern, and always use the strategy called Giving Effective Commands.*

Oppositional Defiant Disorder

Another intense type of defiance that erupts during the preschool years is called Oppositional Defiant Disorder. Its definition and criteria was presented earlier in the chapter. Oftentimes, ODD manifests as frequent and severe tantrums and an intolerance to frustration. This is a diagnostic label in the *DSM-IV* under Behavior Disorders. As a disorder, it requires adjustments to the relationship with the caregivers, environmental modifications and the services of a qualified professional.

So how do we determine when the behavioral traits of a child warrant a diagnostic label and professional intervention or are simply signs of her temperament that warrants adjustments to the adult-child relationship or environment? The sorting out can be very challenging, but the answer may lie in this statement: A criterion for diagnostic label is met only when the behavior occurs more frequently than is typically observed in individuals of comparable age and developmental level, and the disturbance causes clinically significant impairment in social, academic, or occupational functioning. However, according to the research by the National Research Council Institute of Medicine, "The absence of a nationally representative epidemiological study of mental health problems in the childhood population leaves us in the dark with regard to efforts to distinguish children who are at the ends of a typical spectrum from those who are manifesting serious delays."[39]

---

* Giving Effective Commands is covered in chapter 11.

From this information, we conclude that for some children, the behavioral patterns become the symptoms of a disturbance, while for others, they are not. We may also conclude that systems working with children and families differ. Some are based on pathology, diagnosis and treatment, while others are based on prevention, wellness and teaching. What is critical to keep in your frame of reference is that individual styles are not necessarily disorders, and they should not be treated as such.

In too many instances, the lack of differentiation between temperament traits and disorders has resulted in over-diagnosis, misdiagnosis and ineffective treatment. For example, the prevalence of Attention Deficit Disorder with Hyperactivity ranges from 3-7% of the school-age population. However, in some states, the rate of diagnosis reaches as high as 21-33%. This begs the question. With the percentage of "I" children in the population at 30% and the traits of this type and ADHD bearing some similarities, could it be possible that this apparent over-diagnosis not be related to a neurological dysfunction at all, but rather to the child's behavioral or developmental profile? It must also be remembered that all young children display limited or poor impulse control and attention span.

When a person is diagnosed and therapeutic services are recommended, it is important to acknowledge that people have different preferences and personalities, and therefore there are different pathways to healing. Not all individuals benefit from talk therapy or play therapy. Not all individuals benefit from individual therapy. For example, "C" type individuals generally prefer self-help books, self-assessment and personality tools, and retreats. "I" types frequently prefer support groups, creative movement and Outward Bound type programs. "S" types prefer journals and music therapy. "D" types see themselves as never needing therapy and will be the most difficult to engage. Understanding DISC and matching the type of therapeutic intervention to the person's profile increases the effectiveness of and satisfaction with the treatment.

Having read the records of thousands of children, it has been noted that for those with behaviors that challenge their provider or educator, the record becomes nothing more than ongoing documentation of each child's "problems or failures." Notations are given such as, "Morgan had a difficult day. He bit three children. He is an angry child," become the record and how the child is known. The reality of the situation is that Morgan probably had a typical day. The teacher and the children bitten had the difficult day. Morgan may use the biting behavior to express frustration and anger, because he lacks more constructive skills.

From my experience, the records of children with behavioral concerns become a documentation of failure. When in reality, it better serves the child when we prevent this failure from occurring in the first place. When we notice a child is spontaneous and label it as impulsivity, it is not sufficient to write it somewhere and talk about the problems created as a result of this trait. We now must accept the responsibility to teach the skill the child lacks. This skill is impulse control. In addition, when a child is referred to as being angry, we hold the responsibility to teach anger management skills. The label should never define the whole child. It should refer only to the child's deficits or weaknesses.

As we study the DISC model and mental health in greater depth, we realize that each type has areas we should closely watch. The following diagram highlights these areas.

D	I
Anger	Anger
Defiance	Impulsivity
Hostility	Distractibility
Oppositionality	Lack of Self-Discipline
High Energy Level	High Energy Level

C	S
Worry	Fear
Self-Condemnation	Procrastination
Depression	Anxiety
Obsession/Compulsion	Withdrawal

Whether diagnosed or not, children need to learn new skills to minimize their areas of weakness. In the realm of self-regulation, there are three tasks: (1) emotions regulation (2) energy and impulse regulation (3) attention regulation. As you look at the weaknesses in each personality style section, note that the weaknesses of the "Ds" and "Is" have more potential to cause problems in the classroom. Thus, it is not surprising that greater numbers of "D" and "I" children have been referred to me.

"D" and "I" children frequently need help in learning to handle their emotions. "D" children benefit from learning anger management skills and ways to modulate the intensity of their emotional expressions. They need practice with impulse control, flexible thinking and appropriately expressing their feelings and thoughts. While "I" children have difficulty being distracted and causing others to be distracted. "I" children need to learn how to break tasks into smaller components, remove distractions, stay on task and organize tasks.

For the "C" and "S" children, we hold an obligation to teach relaxation and coping strategies to help them manage their fearful, anxious or worrisome nature and negative thought patterns. Because of their preference to the internal world, it would be beneficial to teach play skills, particularly ways to initiate and join into play. "C" and "S" children will benefit from instruction in assertiveness. Nevertheless, it needs to be noted that being shy and reserved is a natural part of their nature and should not be seen as a problem.

In today's world, we are hearing a lot about what we should be teaching children and many say that we should get back to the basics. The basics, in the context of the educational milieu, refer to the teaching of reading, writing and arithmetic. However, in the context of mental health and behavior, the basics are teaching self - regulation and self - discipline and the first precedes the latter. Therefore, in your work with children, identify what skill the child lacks, develop a plan to teach it, and provide sufficient opportunities for practice. In the process of teaching, recognize there is always a struggle on the part of the learner.

At one of my training exercises, I invited a volunteer to come up to the front of the group. (I chose a high "I" woman, because "Is" enjoy being in front of people, and they generally do not mind looking foolish as long as people are giving them attention.) I placed three rubber balls, approximately two inches in diameter, into this woman's hands. I then instructed her to juggle the three balls as she has seen folks do at the circus or on television. (I knew that the chances were slim that this woman could juggle.)

In her attempt to juggle, the balls scattered around the room. Some of the audience (generally the "Ss") stared in compassionate silence, while the rest laughed at her failed attempt to juggle.

In order to make the "Ss" feel more comfortable, I told the woman, "None of us would be able to do any better. You are a great sport to try." I then continued by saying, "Now, I am going to give you an easier assignment. I want you to juggle two balls." I then handed the woman two balls. As she successfully juggled the balls, I said, "Audience, let's give a hand to this great sport!!" The audience then cheers and claps.

This activity was designed to help the audience visually see a key point. I wanted them to understand that as we learn new skills, there will be a struggle, but that struggle does not mean failure. Growth comes from the struggle. As in the juggling illustration, the struggle must not be completely removed. However, in planning to teach, we must consider at what level of skill the child can experience enough success to want to stay in the struggle and practice until mastery is achieved. How long will this process take? There are no guarantees. We just need to keep teaching and providing opportunities to practice, with encouragement and positive feedback for as long as it takes.

CHAPTER 13

WHAT DO YOU NEED?

"What people want is to be heard and seen for who they are."

Mariaemma Willis and Victoria Kindle Hudson [40]

13

There is a principle that says when needs are met, people flourish. When needs are not met, people struggle, and their behaviors become difficult to manage. These negative behaviors communicate that something is not right. Children know when they need something, but they may not know or be able to articulate what they need.

According to L. Tobin, in the book, *What Do You Do With A Child Like This?*, children bring to us needs that must be met within the first hour of the day or at the beginning of our time with them. He refers to these needs as First Hour Needs. [41] The premise of this concept is that when we create an environment for children so that their needs get met, the rest of the day goes more smoothly for everyone. However, if we choose to ignore these needs, we will fight the behaviors that are symptomatic of the unmet need for the rest of the day.

Overview of First Hour Needs

HUMOR	COMMUNICATION
ACKNOWLEDGEMENT	STRUCTURE
TOUCH	PHYSICAL ACTIVITY
NUTRITION	RELAXATION
ENCOURAGEMENT	SOCIALIZATION

HUMOR

For some children, humor is very serious business. Humor can be a stress buffer and a positive coping strategy. Research suggests that individuals who use humor suffer less fatigue, tension, anger and depression.

Morgan

When this need for humor is not met, a child may use his behaviors to bring humor to the environment. I was called to observe a child in a classroom for his sexual behaviors. After one hour and twenty minutes of observation, I had not seen anything. The child that I was observing, a five-year-old boy named Morgan, was nicely playing with two other boys in the block area.

After an hour and twenty minutes, Morgan walked over to the dramatic play area where three girls were playing. He asked them what they were doing, and the answer came back. "We're playing house."

Morgan then asked, "Can you be anything you want?" Gaining an affirmative answer, he then reassigned each child a role. One was the mommy, the second was the sister and the last was the baby. He was now the dad.

Morgan pointed to the child who was the mommy and said, "Now, make me breakfast."

My first thought was, "It's a good thing he does not live in my house, because those demands would get him nowhere." Nevertheless, the child happily began to make him breakfast. It consisted of spaghetti, coffee and scrambled eggs. As the young cook began to whip up the scrambled eggs, Morgan tapped her on the shoulder and when she turned around, he pulled his pants down to expose his bottom. I classify that behavior as mooning. So on my observation form, I wrote the word "mooning" and placed the number one after it.

After forty-five minutes had passed without incident, the

announcement came that lunch was ready. Once all the children and teachers arrived at the lunch table, Morgan started telling "dirty jokes." At his young age, Morgan had no way of understanding the content of those jokes. But, it appeared that he heard an adult telling the jokes and to the best of his ability, he was retelling them to his friends.

While I was consulting with the teacher later that afternoon, I asked her, "Why do you think Morgan did what he did?" She replied that she did not know. I then asked, "Well, what happened when he exposed his bottom to the girls?"

"They laughed."

"And what happened when he told the jokes at the lunch table?"

A light came on in the teacher's eyes as she replied, "PEOPLE LAUGHED!"

I share this story of Morgan, because he uses humor to bring lightness to his life. When the environment does not have humor, children will frequently create laughter in any way that they have been taught in order to meet that need. My counsel to the teacher was to increase the experiences with humor in the classroom in order to teach Morgan, and the other children, appropriate ways to include humor in their day.

ACKNOWLEDGEMENT

Acknowledgement is the greeting we provide to children to welcome them into a new day. It delivers the message that we recognize you as part of our community, whether the community is a family or a classroom, and we are glad you are with us. A child who is seeking acknowledgement may demand your attention throughout the day. This demand for acknowledgement may sound like, "Do you still love me? Am I being good? Will I get a sticker today?" The child is looking for someone to connect with, so our responsibility is to ensure that he has someone to connect with and he knows that he is valued.

One of the ways we do this is to greet each child using his name. It is also suggested that the greeter have a smile on her face, so the child knows she is happy to see him. I mention this because there are adults who have chosen to work with children, yet maintain an attitude that can be referred to as being "weaned on a pickle." Rarely do these adults smile or show enthusiasm toward the children they serve. Therefore, a "weaned on a pickle" greeting consists of a serious expression or furrowed brow, or no acknowledgement at all that the child has arrived. When greeted, the adult begins to spew directives and orders like, "Hang up your coat and backpack. Sit at your seat. Take out your work. Use your walking feet."

When group meetings happen, the "weaned on a pickle" attitude leads to these directives, "Sit criss-cross apple sauce, like a pretzel, on your rug square." When I hear teachers say those words, it makes me wonder how many of the children know that pretzels do not sit? In fact, I once heard a teacher say those words, and I then observed one of the children lean over and bite the child next to him. The reason was clear to me. The teacher had just described children as pretzels, and what do you do with pretzels?

Another directive that I have seen be misunderstood by children is, "Zip your lips, and lock them shut. Now, throw away the key." When was the last time you were able to find a zipper on your lips or a lock for that matter?

The point of this section is that children need acknowledgement delivered in a way they can understand it, and they need to know that they are an important part of our lives.

TOUCH

This need was addressed in the earlier chapter on nurturance styles and love languages. As a review, remember that a child who needs touch will seek it by touching others.

Bobby

Bobby was a child in need of touch. The way he communicated his need was through rough - housing. He was in search of other children who would wrestle with him. When he could not find a wrestling buddy, he would bump into things and people, as though he was a bumper car. His teacher, Mrs. Tanner was heard saying, "Bobby, keep your hands and feet to yourself. Respect his space." During one observation, I heard his name and this reminder eight times in a fifteen minute period.

As I explained to the teacher, the goal becomes teaching Bobby how to meet his need, rather than denying the need and suppressing the behavioral indicators. For example, adults in Bobby's life can help curb Bobby's craving for touch by greeting him with a high - five or a hug.

NUTRITION

According to Maslow's hierarchy of needs, hunger is one of the most basic needs. The following represents the hierarchy.

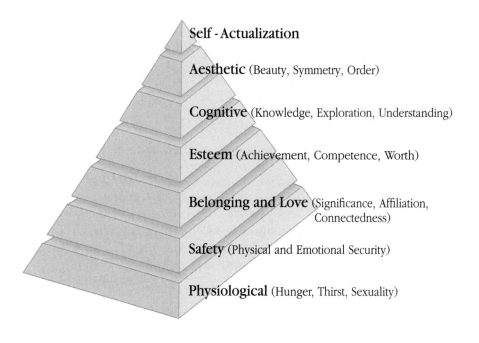

Self - Actualization

Aesthetic (Beauty, Symmetry, Order)

Cognitive (Knowledge, Exploration, Understanding)

Esteem (Achievement, Competence, Worth)

Belonging and Love (Significance, Affiliation, Connectedness)

Safety (Physical and Emotional Security)

Physiological (Hunger, Thirst, Sexuality)

The premise behind this theory is that if the basic needs of children are not met, it becomes increasingly more difficult or impossible to address the higher level needs that are necessary for successful learning and healthy relationships. For example, children who are hungry are focused on finding food to fill their stomachs. Therefore, children will steal food and hoard it in response to their hunger need.

One of the more common problems today, is that many children are not getting proper nutrition. They are fed foods with empty calories because of convenience. For example, Susie came to school very excited to report that her dad stopped to buy her a donut for breakfast today. By 9:30, she was whining, because she was hungry.

There are also cultural influences that affect nutrition. Recently, I had the opportunity to work with a child who was complaining about her belly hurting. This complaint was heard each day. Her teacher, Mrs. Rogers, thought the problem might be connected to stress or anxiety. However, upon further assessment, it was discovered that in the family's culture, females are not allowed to eat at the same time or in the company of males. The males eat first and when there is food remaining, the females can eat. This child was the only female child in a family of seven. Oftentimes, she did not eat, because her father and older brothers ate what was available before she and her mother could eat.

The examples in this section highlight the fact that there may be many reasons that the physiological need for hunger is not getting met. First Hour Needs requires us to acknowledge these facts and feed the child.

ENCOURAGEMENT

A child seeking encouragement will demand reassurance or adopt what is referred to as an attitude of "assumed inadequacy." This child may respond with "I can't do it," before trying to do something.

Emily

Children need adults in their life that recognize what they do well and lead them down the pathway to success. Mrs. Wong was that adult for one child, Emily. Emily wrote, "One of my favorite people who helped me develop one of my better talents is my fourth grade teacher. Mrs. Wong is off the charts, extraordinary in every way. Whenever she comes into the room, I feel like I'm the luckiest kid in the whole world. She always makes me laugh when I am down or upset, and she always has a smile on her face. Mrs. Wong also loves my writing. She always talks to me and tells me that I will be an author one day. 'Emily T. Smith, famous author!' she says. She makes me believe it! She is a teacher, a second mom, a big sis and a best friend all in one. She is my teacher, and I shall never forget her and what she did for me." This illustration portrays the essence of encouragement.

COMMUNICATION

Children whose First Hour Need is communication usually wake up and the first thing out of their mouth is, "Mom, can I tell you something? I just gotta tell you one thing…" The difficulty with this statement is that the one thing can continue for forty-five minutes or more, and it interrupts the rest of the schedule.

Some children are dealing with environments that are not physically or emotionally safe, and they have information to get off their chest. A little girl named Abby told me one day, "You know my daddy, Kenny. He's not a very good daddy. You know, he hurts my mommy and the police come. Sometimes, he hurts me, and I cry."

These stories break your heart, but there are children who need to tell them. So what can we do to provide a listening ear? One strategy being used is called Daily News. As children enter the environment, an adult asks them if they have any daily news they would like to share. A notation is written on a piece of paper or newsprint paper. Within the first hour of the day, the adult then engages the child in a conversation about the news.

STRUCTURE

Predictability and order in an environment provide children with a sense of safety and stability. This sense of safety is the second level in Maslow's hierarchy of needs. In order to effectively meet this need, the structure must be clear. Structure is created through our expectations, schedules and routines. Once structure is established, it must be consistently implemented.

PHYSICAL ACTIVITY

On more than one occasion, a parent has asked, "How can I keep my child from getting up so early and getting into everything? He wakes up at 5:30 a.m., and from that moment until he goes to bed at 8 p.m., he doesn't stop long enough to take a breath. He's in constant motion. What can I do?"

At this point in the book, it should come as no surprise that some children have a greater need to move than others. Over the course of my career, I have recommended that children have opportunities to move, not just outdoors, but in the indoors as well. The need for physical activity cannot be delayed until the outdoor time falls into the schedule.

Increasing gross motor opportunities (physical activities that involve the large muscles of the body) indoors does not require letting children throw balls in a classroom or allowing them to run crazy around the room. But it might include stretching activities or dancing. Children may also enjoy playing games like Twister or Charades. There are some children who will not enjoy 12-piece wood puzzles or 500-piece jigsaw puzzles, but can benefit from floor puzzles, because they can crawl while they assemble them.

One strategy we have found particularly useful in early education is called "Movement of the Day." Together, the children and teacher decide how they will transition or move from one activity time to the next. For example, they may decide to move to circle time from choice time by crawling. They may move from the circle to the story area by doing the crab walk. Not only do these movements increase the physical activity opportunities, while ensuring safety, they also reinforce the physical therapy plans for children who may be identified as needing this support.

The bottom line is that we are wiser to channel the energies and physical activity needs into acceptable movement experiences than to try to deal with children who are jumping off the furniture, wrestling on the floor or throwing objects around a room.

RELAXATION

There is a strong connection between body and mind. This means that psychological and emotional reactions directly affect our physical health and well-being. When we think calm thoughts, we are more likely to experience a state of serenity. When we think angry thoughts, we are more likely to experience a state of tension.

There are personality styles that are better adept at relaxation. These children wake up in the morning and are slow to warm up to the world. They may be described as dawdlers or procrastinators. Through the DISC model, we have identified these types by the letters "S" and "C". Their First Hour Need may be relaxation. And if this is true, providing additional time in the morning schedule affords them what they need to warm up and get themselves moving.

Miguel

In Miguel's house, the morning schedule and routines are very chaotic. There are four children. The house has only one bathroom that they must share. The children and parents fight over who will be first in the shower and how long each one takes to get ready in the bathroom. Yelling and anger are pervasive and the result is that all of them leave the house feeling stressed out. Miguel comes to school and all he wants to do is have some peace and quiet. Since there are no spaces designated for this, he isolates himself and cries. The other children call him a baby, because he is crying.

Recognizing the First Hour Need for relaxation would mandate that Miguel have soft, quiet, cozy spaces to go to and pull himself together. It might also mean that the day begins with relaxation activities.

SOCIALIZATION

Some children start their day with a need for play and interaction with their peers. These children may not have a chance to play, because there are no other children in their neighborhood or they may be an only child. Others do not live in safe neighborhoods and cannot play in the yard or on the playground unsupervised. Still others live in homes where the parents encourage quiet, passive activities. As a result, this child may lack social skills and not know how to make friends. This creates a catch 22; the child has a need for friendship and socialization but lacks the skills to become successful at this endeavor.

To support this need, adults might create opportunities for working in pairs. One such strategy is called "Cooperation Days." On cooperation days, there is a particular activity that can only be done in pairs or small groups. For example, Tuesdays are the days for cooperative painting. A piece of paper may be put into a large, empty coffee can. The two children decide what color paints to add to the can. The cover of the can is then taped on. The children sit 6-7 feet apart and the can is rolled from one child to the other. After 4-5 rolls, the can is opened and the cooperative painting is revealed.

CHAPTER 14

DON'T POP YOUR CORK

"I am officially tendering my resignation as an adult. I have decided I would like to accept the responsibilities of childhood again.

I want to go to McDonald's and think that it is a four star restaurant. I want to sail sticks across a fresh mud puddle and make mud pies.

I want to think M&Ms are better than money, because you can eat them. I want to lie under a big oak tree and run a lemonade stand on a hot day.

I want to return to a time when life was simple; when all I knew was colors, nursery rhymes, and my name, but that didn't bother me, because I didn't know that I didn't know and I didn't care. All I knew was to be happy, because I was blissfully unaware of all the things that should make me worried or upset.

I want to think the world is fair and everyone is honest and kind. I want to believe that anything is possible. I want to be oblivious to the complexities of life and overly excited by the little things again.

I want to live simply. I don't want my day to consist of mountains of paperwork, depressing news, gossip, illness, or violence.

I want to believe in the power of smiles, hugs, a kind word, truth, peace, justice, dreams, the imagination, mankind, and making angels in the snow.

So...here's my checkbook and my car keys, my credit cards and bills, my 401K statements. I am officially resigning from adulthood. And if you want to discuss this further, you'll have to catch me first, cause...... Tag! You're it."

Author Unknown

14

We have been talking about the needs of children, but if adults do not take care of their own needs, they cannot adequately deal with the needs of children.

Working with children is demanding at times, yet it is one of the most rewarding experiences that we will ever encounter on this earth. This book is full of ideas that can help people who work with children, but the glue that will enable adults to use these suggestions is each adult's ability to take care of himself or herself.

Adults who work with children are called upon to maintain a state of wellness. Wellness refers to a general state of well-being in all areas of life. These areas are illustrated in the Wheel of Wellness.

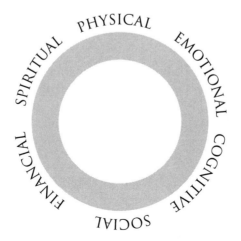

This chapter is dedicated to helping you, the reader, walk through each area of the Wheel of Wellness. This will help you to increase and evaluate how effectively you are handling each area. It will help you to highlight ways to increase your performance.

Look at the wheel on the previous page. As you look at this wheel, reflect on areas that may need attention in your life. Then design a plan.

For many of us, we are moving toward our destination, but it is not smooth. Either the ride is bumpy or we are burning more fuel than necessary, because our engine needs a tune up.

Part of my job in the educational field has been to provide training that helps teachers and parents get tuned up, and then I guide them to remove hindrances blocking their progress. I frequently do the following activity in my training sessions: I give each person a piece of paper cut in a heart shape. (The plan needs to be written on the heart.) Each participant is also given a quilting pin and a cork. Once the plan is written, each person is instructed to pin the plan onto the cork, so that the cork is the base that the heart stands on. Each day, every individual is to commit to doing one thing on their plan, so they move closer to wellness.

PHYSICAL WELLNESS

Physical wellness results from incorporating physical activity or exercise into your lifestyle, maintaining a healthy diet and sleep schedule, and monitoring physical and dental health through recommended visits to your primary care physician and dentist.

Physical activity

Numerous studies have confirmed that an active lifestyle increases longevity by warding off diseases such as strokes, high blood pressure, heart attacks, diabetes, osteoporosis and obesity. In addition, physical exercise increases coping abilities and work productivity. It also decreases the risk of depression. Yet, even with this overwhelming and convincing research, too often we rationalize why we cannot exercise.

- "I have too much on my plate today. I'll start tomorrow."
- "I have a bad back."
- "I can't afford the membership fee."

- "It's too cold outside today."
- "I hate to sweat."
- "It's not fun!"
- "I've never been good at sports."

Whatever the excuses, it is important to eliminate them and include physical activity in our schedule. Consider increasing the amount of physical activity and exercise that you receive. It does not have to be time intensive or cause pain. Simple changes help. For example, walking the stairs instead of taking an elevator, or parking further away from the entrance to a building. Often, simple lifetime changes can include playing active games with your children (such as jumping rope or playing a game of wiffle ball), bike riding, gardening, swimming or hiking. If these are too strenuous, perhaps low intensity aerobics or Pilates will suit your style. Whatever your choice, make sure to choose an activity that is enjoyable, convenient and within your budget. Be sure to discuss your plan with your physician.

Maintaining a healthy diet

Maintaining proper nutrition and a healthy relationship to food may necessitate some changes in your habits. To gain an awareness of your eating habits, write down everything that you eat for five days, right after you eat it. As you are writing, include what you were doing while eating and whom you were with at the time. In addition, record your mood or how you were feeling.

At the end of the five days, analyze the recordings. You may notice that your unhealthy eating happens at a particular time of the day, such as when you are watching television or driving in the car. Or you may uncover that you overeat when feeling stressed or bored. Once identified, you can create a plan to adjust your habits and move toward a more healthful lifestyle.

Maintaining a healthy sleep schedule

According to research, most of us experience an occasional sleepless night of tossing and turning. There are significant effects from losing sleep. The main ones are feeling sleepy, foggy thinking and irritability. These effects may impact your tolerance for the playful noises heard while children are playing. It might also affect the patience you can muster while helping children work through their squabbles. Therefore, it is recommended that you reflect on your sleep habits and the behaviors that disrupt your sleep pattern in the same way that you examined your eating habits. For example, do you have difficulty falling asleep or staying asleep because of stress or worry? Is your sleep of good or poor quality? Do you oversleep or have an inconsistent sleep schedule? Once your sleep awareness is enhanced, create a plan for healthy adjustments. You may need to turn the television off at least one hour before sleep to relax your mind. Or it may be that you get too little exercise. Or, your environment may not be conducive to sleep, so you may decide to change the temperature, light or noise levels.

A commitment to your health may be one of the greatest investments you can make as a parent or provider. Not only will you function more efficiently in this role but you will become a better role model to all those children you love.

EMOTIONAL WELLNESS

It is important to commit ourselves to educating our emotions, because emotions (such as anger, sadness, guilt, fear and worry) interfere with our ability to cope with the demands of parenting and teaching. Research confirms that 60 – 80 % of illnesses are emotionally induced. Every emotion reveals itself in the body. For example, when we are angry, blood rushes to our hands, and we may feel tension. The need to release this tension may result in clenching our fists or feeling like slapping a child. Therefore, re-educating the physical body through exercise, diet and a commitment to your health is an important part of the equation to wellness.

It has been said that it's not what happens to you but how you respond to what happens to you that really matters. Our attitude can make or break us. Here is a story I retrieved from the Internet:

Michael is the kind of guy you love to hate. He is always in a good mood and always has something positive to say. When someone would ask him how he was doing, he would reply, "If I were any better, I would be twins!"

Michael is a natural motivator. If an employee was having a bad day, Michael was there telling the employee how to look on the positive side of the situation.

Seeing this style really made me curious, so one day I went up to Michael and asked him, "I don't get it! You can't be a positive person all of the time. How do you do it?"

Michael replied, "Each morning I wake up and say to myself, 'You have two choices today. You can choose to be in a good mood...or you can choose to be in a bad mood.' I choose to be in a good mood. Each time something happens, I can choose to be a victim or...I can choose to learn from it. I choose to learn from it. Every time someone comes to me complaining, I can choose to accept their complaining...or I can point out the positive side of life. I choose the positive side of life."

"Yeah, right, it's not that easy," I protested.

"Yes, it is," Michael said. "Life is all about choices. When you cut away all the junk, every situation is a choice. You choose how you react to situations. You choose how people affect your mood. You choose to be in a good mood or bad mood. The bottom line is it's your choice how you live your life."

I reflected on what Michael said. Soon thereafter, I left the industry to start my own business. We lost touch, but I often think about him when I make a choice *about* life instead of *reacting* to it.

Several years later, I heard that Michael was involved in a serious accident, falling some 60 feet from a communications tower. After 18 hours of surgery and weeks of intensive care, Michael was released from the hospital with rods placed in his back.

I saw Michael about six months after the accident. When I asked him how he was, he replied, "If I were any better, I'd be twins. Wanna see my scars?" I declined to see his wounds, but I did ask him what had gone through his mind as the accident took place.

"The first thing that went through my mind was the well-being of my soon-to-be-born daughter," Michael replied. "Then, as I lay on the ground, I remembered that I had two choices: I could choose to live or... I could choose to die. I chose to live."

"Weren't you scared? Did you lose consciousness?" I asked.

Michael continued, "The paramedics were great. They kept telling me I was going to be fine. But when they wheeled me into the ER and I saw the expressions on the faces of the doctors and nurses, I got really scared. In their eyes, I read, 'He's a dead man.' I knew I needed to take action."

"What did you do?" I asked.

"Well, there was a big burly nurse shouting questions at me," said Michael. "She asked if I was allergic to anything. 'Yes,' I replied. The doctors and nurses stopped working as they waited for my reply. I took a deep breath and yelled, 'Gravity.' Over their laughter, I told them, 'I am choosing to live. Operate on me as if I am alive, not dead.'"

Michael lived, thanks to the skill of his doctors, but also because of his amazing attitude. I learned from him that every day we have the choice to live fully. Attitude, after all, is everything.

Overcoming Adversity

So often in my work, I encounter folks who have been beaten down by the circumstances in their life. When I ask how they are doing, they reply, "Well, under the circumstances..." This is followed by a litany of problems and adversities.

When I get that answer, my first thought is, "What are you doing under the circumstances? Don't you realize your potential is far greater than any circumstance that will enter your world? Use your talents to stretch beyond your current limitations and soar beyond the obstacles."

When I face adversity, I can choose to live under the circumstances or... I can choose to live above the circumstances with a positive attitude and change what I can change. In addition, when overcoming adversity, having a sense of humor is helpful. Humor is the medicine for the soul. To support the development of a funny bone, read and collect cartoons, joke books, or humorous magazines. Visit a comedy club or watch a funny video. I have learned that doing something unexpected can produce fun and humor.

One day I was sitting in traffic at a tollbooth, just outside Boston. Horns were beeping, and people were rolling down their windows to gesture and yell at the cars in front of them. It was prime opportunity for road rage. Having just finished presenting to educators on the topic of stress, I reached into the container on the back seat of my car and pulled out a bottle of bubbles. I rolled down the driver's side window and began blowing bubbles.

The car behind me started honking again. The gentleman in the car to the left gave me a look of disgust. It was clear to me that my actions were not appreciated. The car behind the one to may left slowly moved up in the line and once beside me, rolled down his window and asked if I had another bottle of bubbles. As a result, now two of us were filling the air with bubbles. Whether appreciated or not, there was nothing we could do to control the flow of traffic. So we chose to change our frame of mind and enjoy the circumstances we were in at the time.

Remember not to take yourself or life too seriously. Our time is short, and this is not a dress rehearsal. The show must go on, and we are more satisfied and less stressed when we bring humor with us onto the stage of life.

Affirmation

Affirm yourself! An affirmation is a positive thought or saying. When I do training, I teach people to use affirmations. In one program that I did in a school, I implemented a strategy called "Just a Thought." Each week, a positive thought was sent out on designer paper to all the teachers. In my instructions to the teachers, I asked them to reflect upon the meaning that the thought had in regard to their work with children.

Examples of these thoughts are:

You cannot cancel out your own faults by pointing out the faults of others.

You cannot change the color of a child's eyes, but you can make them glow with the light of your love.

When faced with problems or when feeling stress, it is helpful to think cheerful, positive thoughts that will uplift you and make the difficult path seem easier. Therefore, I will say positive affirmations when I enter a difficult situation. For example, as I approach a child who is misbehaving, I think, "I can handle this. It is another opportunity to teach, and I am an effective teacher. I have taught this to hundreds of children." Another affirmation I have used is, "This will pass, but in the meantime, I am doing my best every day."

A Support System

Emotional wellness is enhanced through a good support system. Who are the people we surround ourselves with? Are they uplifting, playful and encouraging? Or are they "crabs in a bucket?" You will know a crab in the bucket by the messages he or she delivers. A crab in the bucket will have you believing less about yourself than you were designed to be. They drag you down into the muck and mire.

The term "crab in a bucket" comes from nature. When one crab is placed in a bucket, it can escape the confines of the bucket by crawling out. When two or more crabs are placed in the bucket, they cannot escape. When one begins to climb out, another crab will pull it back down. There are people, like crabs, who go through life pulling others down. Their fear does not allow them to support the growth and success of others. Instead, they are comfortable with mediocrity and conformity.

When I do training, I frequently emphasize the significance of having a support system through an activity I call "Balcony People." Each participant in the workshop is handed two toothpicks. Once the toothpicks have been handed out, each person is instructed to take one of the toothpicks and get it to stand upright without holding it, balancing it with a finger or making a hole in the table. The toothpick must stand freely. After several attempts without success, each participant is asked to pick the toothpick up, holding each end between the thumb and forefinger of the right and left hands. Now, snap the toothpick in half. All feel the success of snapping the toothpick without a struggle.

Now, beginning with one participant in the left front of the group, have him pass his toothpick to the person sitting on his right, then that individual passes his toothpick to his right and so on until all of the toothpicks are in the hands of the person sitting in the last seat of last row. The person is holding an elastic band and is instructed to wrap the elastic around the bundle of toothpicks. Once completed, she is asked to stand the bundle of toothpicks up on the table without support. This time, there is success in short order. "Now, take the bundle in your hands and snap it in half." There is no success, because the bundle is too thick.

This is what our support system becomes to us in times of stress. When we try to stand alone, we may fall over and snap. But when joined together, we gather strength and weather the storm. Having that support is not a sign of weakness, but great strength - so use your support network. As former First Lady and now Senator Hilary Rodham Clinton wrote, "It takes a village to raise a child."

COGNITIVE WELLNESS

Cognitive refers to our perception about things and how we think about what we perceive. Our thoughts influence our feelings and moods, which in turn, influence our actions.

There are ten thought patterns that can rob us of experiencing wellness.

1. Overgeneralization. "He never listens to a thing I tell him," or "Why does this always happen to me?"

2. Black and white thinking. A child is either very, very good, or he is very, very bad. There is no in between.

3. Personalization. For example, when your child does not do his homework, and you take the blame. "Please excuse Elaine for not having her homework done. It is my fault. We had unexpected company drop by, and I did not have time to sit with her."

4. Awfulizing. "Oh no. This is awful. I can't believe this is happening to me. Why now?"

5. Discounting the positive. Your child says, "You're a great mom," and you think she must be buttering you up, because she wants something.

6. Labeling. When you make a mistake, you give yourself a negative label. For example, you call yourself stupid. "I can't believe I let myself get sucked into that argument again. How stupid of me! When will I ever learn?"

7. Magnification. For example, when you are on your way to pick up your child at school and you get stuck in rush hour traffic, you think, "I can't deal with this." The reality is that you must deal with it, because you have no control over it.

8. Mental filter. You have taken a test and did not know the answer to one question. Your score was 98%. Instead of focusing on the success, you focus on the answer you did not know and the loss of 2 points.

9. Should, Have To, Must and Ought To. These types of thoughts increase pressure and stress. "Good teachers should go to their student's dance recital." Instead, use the words: I choose to, I want to or I get the privilege of.

10. Emotional reasoning. I just broke my promise with my child, and I feel awful. Therefore, because I feel awful, I must be an awful parent and not trustworthy.

These 10 distortions of thought must be controlled or eliminated as soon as they enter our awareness.

Nourishing the mind

A question that has crossed my mind on more than one occasion is that we provide food and nutrients to our physical bodies three or more times each day, but how many times do we provide nutrients to our mind? And if we committed ourselves to doing this, what would we be doing?

There are volumes of books and magazines that can feed our minds with valuable information. If you do not like to read, tackle just one page a day out of a book and read that page or listen to the audio version while you are driving in the car. Also, there are numerous seminars, workshops and conferences offered every day by experts in the field of child development, education, relationships and parenting. The cost of these offerings varies greatly, from no charge to hundreds of dollars. There are also catalogues full of training videotapes and DVDs. Whether you are a visual, auditory or hands-on learner, there are opportunities available to you as you commit yourself to professional or personal growth and cognitive wellness.

SOCIAL WELLNESS

I have worked with many parents and professionals that have given up their hobbies, because they lack the time or the resources to indulge themselves. One mom was having suicidal thoughts at the age of twenty-seven, because she was no longer taking care of her own needs. When she became a mom, two years earlier, she felt guilty every time she spent money for a babysitter, so she could play tennis or go out to dinner with her husband. Her mother repeatedly told her, "Good mothers stay home with their children, because no one can care for them as good as you." Over time, the guilt was overbearing. She was a professional woman trying to act as "SUPERMOM, SUPERWIFE, SUPERDAUGHTER and PERFECT EMPLOYEE. She invested all of her energy into maintaining the myth, but forgot to remain true to herself in the process. The solutions to this predicament were found in understanding time management and completing an activity called "Ten Loves," developed by Dr. Sidney B. Simon. (This activity is found later in the chapter.)

Time Management

In time management, this mom was asked to answer four questions before she committed herself to doing a task.

1. Must this be done?

2. Must this be done now?

3. Must this it be done by me?

4. Must this be done their way to please them?

What she discovered was that what she thought she must do *and do now* were actually false beliefs she received from her own upbringing. She then learned the magic of delegation. She also gained wisdom from the story of the professor who was instructing his students about what is really important in life.

As the story goes, a philosophy professor stood before his class with some items on the table in front of him. When the class began, he wordlessly picked up a very large, empty mayonnaise jar and proceeded to fill it with rocks. Each rock was about 2 - 3 inches in diameter. He then asked the students if the jar was full. They agreed that it was.

The professor then picked up a box of pebbles and poured them into the jar. He shook the jar lightly. The pebbles rolled into the open areas between the rocks. He then asked once again if the jar was full. The students responded with a unanimous, "YES."

The professor then produced a jar of sand from under the table and proceeded to pour the entire contents into the jar - effectively filling the empty space between the pebbles and the rocks. The students laughed.

When the laughter subsided, the professor said, "Now, I want you to recognize that this jar represents your life. The rocks are the important things – your family, your partner, your health, your children – the things that if everything else was lost and only they remained, your life would still be full. The pebbles are the other things that matter – like your job, your home and your car. The sand is everything else - the small stuff."

He continued, "If you pour out the sand into the jar first, there is no room for the pebbles and rocks. The same goes for your life. If you spend all your time and energy on the small stuff, you will never have room for the things that are really important to you. Pay attention to the things that are critical to your happiness. Play with your children. Take time to get medical checkups. Take your partner out dancing. Remember, there will always be time to go to work, clean the house, give a dinner party and fix the disposal. Take care of the rocks first – the things that really matter. Set your priorities. The rest is just sand."

The mom I was counseling, had lost sight of the rocks and in particular, her own health. An exercise called "The Ten Loves" helped to bring perspective back to her with regards to her social and recreational needs.

Ten Loves

Take a moment to complete this "Ten Loves" exercise. First, make two columns on a sheet of paper. Then in the left-hand column, write down ten things you love to do. Then to the right of each love, answer these questions:

    a. The date you last did it?

    b. Do you prefer doing this alone or with others?

    c. Would the people that support you approve of you doing this?

    d. How long ago was it that you liked to do this?

    e. Do you expect to do it again, and if so, when?

    f. Does it involve risk or jeopardize your health and safety?

    g. Is your current health status a barrier to doing this?[42]

The last step in this activity is to put a mark next to the five loves you enjoy the most and commit to doing at least one each week.

FINANCIAL WELLNESS

I am not an expert in the area of finances and money management, but I know that financial wellness it is not a matter of how much you earn. What is more important is how much you keep of what you earn. I have also learned that it is costly to pay off one credit card with another and consolidate debt. The third lesson I learned was that living by sound financial principles not only increases your net worth, but it decreases stress.

When we were starting our family, it seemed like the needs were far greater than the resources available. We had a sign hanging in our home that said, "We have more month left at the end of the money."

It is difficult to parent effectively when you are feeling so financially inept. We were working as hard as we could to stay above water and meet the demands, but it seemed like the harder we worked, the more water our ship took on. We were sinking.

If you are drowning in a sea of debt, find a wise financial planner and straighten things out. A wise financial planner is not *working for* and *living by* a weekly paycheck. He is a student of money and the ways to make money work for you.

Through the process of sorting out our finances, I learned a fourth valuable lesson. When you have a passion for your profession and you provide quality service to your consumers, the money becomes a by-product. After learning this lesson, I have shared this thought with many folks. If you cannot have fun doing what you are doing, then do not do it.

Your Career

I have talked to many professionals who hate the work they do every day. As I was speaking to a dad last week, I asked the question, "When thinking about your financial and career life, what would you like to see your child do differently?"

Without hesitation, he replied, "I'd like for him to pick a career that he will enjoy."

As you choose what to do for work, make sure the values of that organization align with your personal values. In the field of education, there are ten core values: quality, inclusion, empowerment, collaboration, learning, advocacy, wellness, nurturing, diversity and continuity. Last year, I coached a teacher out of the profession, because she could not embrace the value of inclusion. She held firmly to the belief that "this child does not belong here." This belief held her back from pursuing individualization and adaptively responding to the needs of the child. She needed to gladly teach him the skills he needed to overcome the behaviors she was so challenged by. In short, the misalignment in values increased her job stress, while decreasing her job satisfaction. Moreover, it became a bone of contention with her supervisor. I informed this teacher that she was a wonderful teacher in so many ways and listed, specifically what those were. We agreed that she should pursue another program where those strengths could be put to good use, and she would experience a better fit with her values and beliefs.

SPIRITUAL WELLNESS

According to *Webster's Seventh Collegiate Dictionary*, being spiritual means "of, relating to, or consisting of spirit." The second explanation is "of or relating to sacred matters." [43]

Although spirituality is related to religion, it encompasses more than the rituals and practices of any particular denomination. In this country, the Constitution protects freedom of religion. And this is as it should be. However, as we talk about the spiritual aspect of our being here, we are referring to the part of the definition that says "relating to sacred matters."

I am of the opinion that the unseen potential of every child and adult is precious. Having a belief and faith in things unseen is sacred. Therefore, our goal is to believe that every child is capable of success. Our efforts must always be directed toward the achievement of that success. And, every moment we have the privilege of being in the company of children, we must work tirelessly toward the fulfillment of their potential. Because, as the song by Whitney Houston states, "I believe that children are our future. Teach them well and let them lead the way." [44]

Resources / End notes

1. From *The Irreducible Needs of Children* by T. Berry Brazelton and Stanley Greenspan. Reprinted by permission of Perseus Books PLC, a member of Perseus Books, L.L.C., XVI - XVII.

2. Reprinted with permission from Roberta Andresen through WARM2Kids, Inc.,www.WARM2KIDS.com.

3. Covey, Stephen R., *The Seven Habits of Highly Effective Families* (New York: Golden Books, 1997), 50-58.

4. Kalil, Carolyn, "Follow Your True Colors to the Work You Love," excerpt from book of the same title. Available from http://www.truecolorscareer.com.

5. Marion, Marian, *Guidance of Young Children* (Englewood Cliffs, New Jersey: Prentice-Hall, Inc., 1995), 5.

6. Brazelton, 7.

7. Reprinted with permission from Gene Bedley at ethicsusa@cox.net An except from the story "Just Say It!" printed in *Chicken Soup for the Soul*, First Edition by Jack Canfield and Mark Victor Hansen. (Deerfield Beach, Florida: Health Communications, Inc., 2001), 151.

8. Leman, Kevin, *The New Birth Order Book: Why You Are the Way You Are* (Grand Rapids, Michigan: Revell Books, September 2004)

9. U.S. Department of Health and Human Services. Promoting Mental Health. Washington, D.C.,: U.S. Government Printing Office, 1997.

10. Chapman, Gary and Ross Campbell, MD., *The Five Love Languages of Children* (Chicago: Northfield Publishing, 1997, 2005)

11. Ibid.

12. Ibid.

13. Ibid.

14. Ibid.

15. Ibid.

16. Reprinted by permission. *Silver Boxes*, Florence Littauer, 1989, W Publishing, A Division of Thomas Nelson, Inc., Nashville, Tennessee. All rights reserved, 4.

17. Karr-Morse, Robin and Meredith S. Wiley, *Ghosts from the Nursery* (New York: The Atlantic Monthly Press, 1997), 129.

18. Used by permission of Dr. Robert Rohm and Personality Insights, Inc.

19. Boyd, Charles, *Different Children, Different Needs* (Sisters, Oregon: Multnomah, 1994).

20. Willis, Mariaemma and Victoria Kindle Hudson, *Discover Your Child's Learning Style* (Roseville, California: Prima Publishing, 1999), 24.

21. Concepts used by permission of Dr. Robert Rohm and Personality Insights, Inc.

22. Willis, 29.

23. Used by permission of Dr. Robert Rohm and Personality Insights, Inc.

24. Willis, 30.

25. Information used by permission of Dr. Robert Rohm and Personality Insights, Inc.

26. Reprinted with permission from the Center for Human Development, Barb Zulin, 62320 Tamarack Springs Lane, Summerville, Oregon 97876.

27. Covey, 216.

28. Greenman, J., *Caring Spaces, Learning Places: Children's Environments That Work* (Redmond, Washington: Exchange Press, Inc.), 36.

29.   From *Developmentally Appropriate Practice*, First Edition by Gestwicki, C. © 1995. Reprinted with permission of Delmar Learning, a Division of Thomson Learning: www.thomsonrights.com.

30.   Isenberg, J.P. & Jalongo, M.R. (2006) *Creative thinking and arts-based learning: Preschool through fourth grade* (4th edition). (Upper Saddle River, NJ: Pearson Education), p. 54.

31.   From *Developmentally Appropriate Practice*, First Edition by Gestwicki, C. © 1995. Reprinted with permission of Delmar Learning, a Division of Thomson Learning: www.thomsonrights.com. Adapted from the work of Elizabeth Jones and Elizabeth Prescott. *Dimensions of Teaching-Learning Environments: A Handbook for teachers in elementary schools and day care centers.* Pasadena, California: Pacific Oaks College, 1984. Reprinted with permission from Betty Jones.

32.   Information used with permission of Dr. Robert Rohm and Personality Insights, Inc.

33.   Courtesy of the Ella Wheeler Wilcox Society, ellawheelerwilcox.org.

34.   Covey, 214.

35.   Rohm, Robert A., *A+ Ideas for Every Student's Success* (Atlanta: Personality Insights, 2003), 147.

36.   Crary, Elizabeth, *Kids Can Cooperate* (Seattle: Parenting Press, Inc., 1984), 102.

37.   Reprinted with permission from the *Diagnostic and Statistical Manual of Mental Disorders*, Fourth Edition (Arlington, Virginia: American Psychiatric Association, 2000), 92-93.

38.   Ibid., 102.

39.   Reprinted with permission from The National Research Council Institute of Medicine, The National Academies, 500 Fifth Street NW Washington, D.C. 20001.

40.   Willis, 31.

41.   Tobin, L., *What Do You Do With A Child Like This?* (Duluth, Minnesota: Whole Person Associates, 1991), 105-129.

42.   Reprinted with permission from Dr. Sidney Simon, Values Press, Hadley, Massachusetts 01035.

43.   *Webster's Seventh New Collegiate Dictionary*, Nineteenth Edition (Springfield, Massachusetts: G & C Merriam Company, 1971), 843.

44.   "Greatest Love of All" written by Michael Masser and Linda Creed, performed by Whitney Houston.

Personality
INSIGHTS
PRESS